C# Mastery: A Comprehensive Guide to Programming in C#

Kameron Hussain and Frahaan Hussain

Published by Sonar Publishing, 2023.

C# MASTERY: A COMPREHENSIVE GUIDE TO PROGRAMMING IN C#

First edition. October 24, 2023.

ISBN: 979-8223379584

Written by Kameron Hussain and Frahaan Hussain.

Table of Contents

2. Low-Code and No-Code Development

3. DevOps and Continuous Integration/Continuous Deployment (CI/CD)

4. Serverless Computing

5. Quantum Computing

6. Ethical and Responsible AI

7. Remote and Distributed Work

8. Cybersecurity and Privacy

Section 19.3: The Role of C# in Emerging Technologies

1. Cross-Platform Development with .NET 5+ and .NET 6

2. Web Development with Blazor

3. Machine Learning with ML.NET

4. Cloud-Native Development with Azure Functions

5. Game Development with Unity

Section 19.4: Community and Open Source Contributions

1. Open Source Initiatives

2. GitHub and the .NET Foundation

3. NuGet and Package Management

4. Stack Overflow and Developer Forums

Chapter 1: Introduction to C

Section 1.1: Getting Started with C

Welcome to the world of C#! In this section, we'll take our first steps into the C# programming language and get you up to speed on the basics. Whether you're a complete beginner or have some programming experience, this chapter will help you get started on your C# journey.

What is C#?

C# (pronounced "C-sharp") is a modern, object-oriented programming language developed by Microsoft. It is a versatile language used for building a wide range of software applications, including desktop applications, web applications, mobile apps, and games. C# is known for its simplicity, readability, and robustness, making it an excellent choice for both beginners and experienced developers.

Why Learn C#?

Before we dive into the technical details, let's briefly discuss why learning C# is a valuable skill:

1. **Versatility**: C# can be used to build applications for various platforms, including Windows, web, and mobile.
2. **Popularity**: C# is widely used in the software development industry, ensuring that learning it opens up numerous job opportunities.
3. **Strong Ecosystem**: C# is part of the .NET ecosystem, which provides a rich set of libraries and tools for development.

4. **Great Tooling**: Visual Studio, Microsoft's integrated development environment (IDE), offers powerful tools for C# development.
5. **Community Support**: C# has a vibrant developer community, so you can find plenty of resources, forums, and tutorials to help you along the way.

Now that you understand the importance of C#, let's move on to setting up your development environment.

Setting Up Your Development Environment

Before you can start writing C# code, you'll need to set up your development environment. Here are the essential steps:

1. Install Visual Studio (or Visual Studio Code)

• Visual Studio is a feature-rich IDE for C# development. You can download it from the official Microsoft website.

• If you prefer a lighter-weight option, Visual Studio Code is a popular choice for C# development and can be extended with C# extensions.

2. Install the .NET SDK

• The .NET Software Development Kit (SDK) is essential for building and running C# applications. You can download it from the .NET website.

3. Verify Your Setup

- Once you've installed the necessary tools, open your IDE (Visual Studio or Visual Studio Code) and create a new C# project to ensure everything is set up correctly.

Your First C# Program

Let's not waste any time and jump right into writing your first C# program. In C#, a simple "Hello, World!" program looks like this:

```
using System;

class Program

{

static void Main()

{

Console.WriteLine("Hello, World!");

}

}
```

In this code: - using System; includes the System namespace, which provides access to standard input and output functionality. - class Program defines a class named Program. - static void Main() is the entry point of your C# program. - Console.WriteLine("Hello, World!"); prints "Hello, World!" to the console.

To run this program, simply click the "Run" button in your IDE.

Exploring the .NET Framework

C# is closely tied to the .NET Framework, a comprehensive platform for building various types of applications. The .NET Framework provides libraries and services that make it easier to develop software. As you progress in your C# journey, you'll become more familiar with these libraries and how to leverage them to build powerful applications.

This concludes our introduction to C#. In the following sections, we'll dive deeper into the language's fundamentals, syntax, and concepts. So, buckle up, and let's continue our C# adventure!

Section 1.2: Setting Up Your Development Environment

In the previous section, we briefly discussed the importance of setting up your development environment for C# programming. Now, let's delve deeper into the steps required to configure your environment properly.

1. Install Visual Studio (or Visual Studio Code)

As mentioned earlier, Visual Studio is a powerful integrated development environment (IDE) for C# development. Here's how to install it:

- Visit the official Visual Studio website[1] and download the version that suits your needs (Community, Professional, or Enterprise).

- Follow the installation instructions provided during the download process.

1. https://visualstudio.microsoft.com/

- Once installed, launch Visual Studio, and you'll be ready to start working with C#.

If you prefer a lighter-weight IDE, Visual Studio Code is an excellent choice. You can install it as follows:

- Download Visual Studio Code[2] from the official website.

- Install Visual Studio Code by following the installation instructions specific to your operating system.

- After installation, open Visual Studio Code, and you can begin working with C# by installing relevant extensions.

2. Install the .NET SDK

The .NET Software Development Kit (SDK) is a fundamental component for C# development. It provides the tools necessary for building, testing, and running C# applications. Here's how to install it:

- Go to the official .NET website[3] and download the .NET SDK for your operating system.

- Follow the installation instructions for your platform to complete the installation process.

- To verify that the .NET SDK is installed correctly, open a terminal or command prompt and run the following command:

---

2. https://code.visualstudio.com/

3. https://dotnet.microsoft.com/download

dotnet—version

This command should display the installed .NET SDK version, confirming that your installation was successful.

3. Verify Your Setup

Once you've installed Visual Studio or Visual Studio Code and the .NET SDK, it's essential to verify that your development environment is correctly configured. Here's a quick check:

Visual Studio

1. Open Visual Studio.
2. Click on "File" > "New" > "Project."
3. Choose a C# project template (e.g., Console App).
4. Click "Create" to create a new project.
5. Write a simple C# program and run it to ensure everything is working as expected.

Visual Studio Code

1. Open Visual Studio Code.
2. Install the C# extension if you haven't already. You can do this by searching for "C#" in the extensions marketplace.
3. Create a new C# project or open an existing one.
4. Write a simple C# program and run it to verify that your setup is correct.

By following these steps, you'll have a fully functional C# development environment ready to use for your projects. In the next sections, we'll dive deeper into the C# language and start writing code to build exciting applications.

Section 1.3: Understanding the C# Language Basics

In this section, we'll explore the fundamental building blocks of the C# programming language. These basics are essential for anyone starting with C# development, and they form the foundation for writing C# code effectively.

1. Variables and Data Types

Variables are used to store data in a C# program. C# is a statically typed language, which means that variables must be declared with a specific data type before they can be used. Common data types in C# include int, float, string, bool, and more. Here's how you declare and initialize variables:

int age = 30; *// An integer variable*

float price = 19.99f; *// A floating-point variable (note the 'f' suffix)*

string name = "John"; *// A string variable*

bool isStudent = **true**; *// A boolean variable*

2. Comments

Comments in C# are used to add explanatory notes within your code. They are ignored by the compiler and exist solely for human readability. Single-line comments start with //, and multi-line comments are enclosed in /* */. Here's an example:

// This is a single-line comment

*/**

This is a

multi-line comment

*/

3. Console Input and Output

You can interact with the user by reading input from the console and displaying output. The Console class provides methods for this purpose. To display text, use Console.WriteLine():

Console.WriteLine("Hello, C#!"); *// Prints "Hello, C#!" followed by a newline*

To read input from the user, you can use Console.ReadLine(). Here's an example:

Console.Write("Enter your name: ");

string userName = Console.ReadLine();

Console.WriteLine($"Hello, {userName}!");

4. Arithmetic Operators

C# supports common arithmetic operators for performing mathematical calculations. These include + (addition), - (subtraction), * (multiplication), / (division), and % (modulus). Here's how you can use them:

int a = 10;

int b = 5;

int sum = a + b; *// 15*

int difference = a - b; *// 5*

int product = a * b; *// 50*

```
int quotient = a / b; // 2

int remainder = a % b; // 0
```

5. Control Flow and Decision Making

Control flow statements allow you to make decisions and control the flow of your program. Common control flow structures include if statements for conditional execution, for and while loops for iteration, and switch statements for multiple branching. Here's an example of an if statement:

```
int num = 10;

if (num > 0)

{

Console.WriteLine("Number is positive.");

}

else if (num < 0)

{

Console.WriteLine("Number is negative.");

}

else

{

Console.WriteLine("Number is zero.");

}
```

6. Functions and Methods

In C#, you can define functions (methods) to encapsulate blocks of code for reuse. Methods are declared using the void keyword for methods that don't return a value, and they can accept parameters. Here's an example:

```
void SayHello(string name)

{

Console.WriteLine($"Hello, {name}!");

}

// Calling the method

SayHello("Alice"); // Prints "Hello, Alice!"
```

These are the fundamental language basics of C#. Understanding these concepts is crucial as they lay the groundwork for more advanced topics as you progress in your C# journey. In the upcoming sections, we'll dive deeper into object-oriented programming and more advanced C# features.

Section 1.4: Writing Your First C# Program

Now that you've learned about variables, data types, comments, console input and output, arithmetic operators, and control flow, it's time to put your knowledge into practice by writing your first C# program. In this section, we'll guide you through the process of creating a simple C# program step by step.

1. Creating a New C# Project

Before you start writing code, you'll need a C# project to work on. We'll demonstrate this using Visual Studio, but you can follow similar steps in Visual Studio Code or any other C# IDE.

1. Open Visual Studio.
2. Click on "File" > "New" > "Project..." to create a new project.
3. In the "Create a new project" dialog, search for "Console App (.NET Core)" or "Console App (.NET)" depending on your version of Visual Studio.
4. Choose the appropriate template, provide a name for your project (e.g., "MyFirstCSharpProgram"), and choose a location to save it.
5. Click the "Create" button to create the project.

2. Writing Your First C# Code

Now that you have a project, it's time to write your first C# code. By default, Visual Studio creates a Program.cs file with a Main method. This method is the entry point of your program.

Here's a simple "Hello, World!" program:

```
using System;

class Program

{

static void Main()

{

Console.WriteLine("Hello, World!");
```

```
}

}
```

In this code: - We include the System namespace, which provides access to the Console class for input and output. - We define a Program class with a Main method. The Main method is where your program starts executing. - Inside the Main method, we use Console.WriteLine to print "Hello, World!" to the console.

3. Running Your Program

To run your C# program in Visual Studio, follow these steps:

1. Ensure that the "MyFirstCSharpProgram" project is selected in the Solution Explorer.
2. Click the "Start" button (a green arrow) or press the F5 key to build and run your program.
3. You should see the output in the console window at the bottom of the Visual Studio IDE, displaying "Hello, World!"

Congratulations! You've just written and executed your first C# program.

4. Experimenting Further

Now that you've created a simple program, take some time to experiment and learn. Try the following:

• Modify the "Hello, World!" string to print a different message.

• Declare and use variables to perform calculations.

- Add conditional statements (e.g., if and else) to create logic in your program.
- Explore different console input and output methods to interact with the user.

As you explore and experiment, you'll gain a better understanding of C# and its capabilities. Don't hesitate to consult documentation and online resources whenever you encounter questions or challenges in your learning journey.

This marks the completion of your first C# program. In the following sections, we'll dive deeper into C# concepts, including object-oriented programming and advanced language features. Keep building and exploring!

Section 1.5: Exploring the .NET Framework

In this section, we will explore the .NET Framework and its significance in C# development. Understanding the .NET Framework is essential as it provides a vast library of classes and functions that you can leverage to build robust and feature-rich applications.

What is the .NET Framework?

The .NET Framework is a comprehensive platform developed by Microsoft for building, deploying, and running various types of applications, including desktop applications, web applications, and services. It provides a common runtime environment, a large class library, and tools for developers to create software.

Key components of the .NET Framework include:

- **Common Language Runtime (CLR)**: The CLR is the runtime environment that manages memory, compiles and executes code, and provides features like automatic memory management (garbage collection) and exception handling.

- **Base Class Library (BCL)**: The BCL is a collection of reusable classes and types that provide a wide range of functionality, from basic data types to advanced features like file I/O, networking, and cryptography.

- **ASP.NET**: For web development, ASP.NET is a part of the .NET Framework that allows developers to build web applications and services using C#.

- **Windows Forms and WPF**: These are UI frameworks for building Windows desktop applications with rich graphical interfaces.

- **ADO.NET**: ADO.NET provides data access to databases, enabling you to interact with relational databases like SQL Server, MySQL, and more.

- **Web Services**: .NET Framework supports the creation and consumption of web services, allowing applications to communicate over the internet.

.NET Framework Versions

Over the years, the .NET Framework has evolved, and several versions have been released. The most notable ones include:

- **.NET Framework 1.0**: The initial release, introduced in 2002.

- **.NET Framework 2.0**: Added significant improvements and features.

- **.NET Framework 3.0 and 3.5**: Introduced Windows Communication Foundation (WCF), Windows Presentation Foundation (WPF), and Windows Workflow Foundation (WF).

- **.NET Framework 4.0**: Brought enhancements and support for parallel programming.

- **.NET Framework 4.5**: Included improvements like async/await, enhanced support for ASP.NET, and more.

- **.NET Framework 4.6 and later**: Continued updates and improvements.

.NET Core and .NET 5+

It's important to note that the .NET Framework has evolved into two distinct paths: .NET Core and .NET 5+.

- **.NET Core**: Introduced as an open-source, cross-platform framework, .NET Core focused on providing a smaller, modular runtime and library that could run on Windows, Linux, and macOS. It was designed for modern application development and was especially well-suited for microservices and cloud-native applications.

- **.NET 5+**: Microsoft has since unified .NET Core and .NET Framework into a single platform called .NET 5 and subsequently .NET 6, .NET 7, and so on. This unified platform retains the cross-platform capabilities of .NET

Core while incorporating the best features of the .NET Framework. It is the future of .NET development.

Building with the .NET Framework

To build applications using the .NET Framework, you typically use development tools like Visual Studio. These tools provide a rich development environment with features for code editing, debugging, and project management.

Additionally, you write your code in C# or other .NET-supported languages, compile it into Intermediate Language (IL) code, and then execute it on the CLR. This architecture allows .NET applications to be platform-independent, making it easier to target different operating systems.

In the next sections of this guide, we will delve deeper into C# programming, exploring advanced topics, object-oriented programming, and more. Understanding the .NET Framework and its capabilities will serve as a strong foundation for your C# development journey.

Chapter 2: Building Your First C# Project

Section 2.1: Creating a Console Application

In this section, we'll dive into creating your first C# project, specifically a console application. Console applications are text-based programs that interact with users through the command-line interface (CLI). They are an excellent starting point for learning C# as they allow you to focus on the basics of the language and logic.

What is a Console Application?

A console application in C# is a program that runs in a command-line terminal or console window. It accepts text input from the user, processes it, and provides text output. Console applications are often used for tasks like data processing, automation, and simple user interactions.

Creating a New Console Application

To create a new console application, follow these steps using Visual Studio:

1. Open Visual Studio.
2. Click on "File" > "New" > "Project..." to create a new project.
3. In the "Create a new project" dialog, search for "Console App (.NET Core)" or "Console App (.NET)" depending on your version of Visual Studio.
4. Choose the appropriate template and give your project a name (e.g., "MyConsoleApp").

5. Choose a location to save your project files, and click the "Create" button.

Understanding the Console Application Template

When you create a new console application, Visual Studio generates some initial code for you. Let's take a look at the key components:

- Program.cs: This file contains the main entry point of your console application. It includes a Main method where your program starts execution.

Here's a simple example of a console application:

```
using System;

class Program

{

static void Main()

{

Console.WriteLine("Hello from MyConsoleApp!");

}

}
```

In this code: - We include the System namespace for access to the Console class. - We define a Program class with a Main method, which is the entry point of our program. - Inside the Main method, we use Console.WriteLine to print "Hello from MyConsoleApp!" to the console.

Running Your Console Application

To run your console application in Visual Studio, follow these steps:

1. Ensure that your console application project is selected in the Solution Explorer.
2. Click the "Start" button (a green arrow) or press the F5 key to build and run your program.
3. You'll see the output in the console window at the bottom of the Visual Studio IDE.

Congratulations! You've created and executed your first C# console application. It's a small step, but an important one on your journey to becoming proficient in C# programming.

In the following sections, we'll explore more about working with variables, data types, and control flow in C#. These fundamental concepts will empower you to build more complex and interactive console applications.

Section 2.2: Working with Variables and Data Types

In this section, we'll delve into the essential concepts of variables and data types in C#. Understanding how to work with variables and knowing the available data types is fundamental to writing effective C# code.

What are Variables?

Variables are placeholders for storing data in your program's memory. They give your program the ability to remember and manipulate information. In C#, variables have a data type that determines what kind of data they can hold, such as integers, floating-point numbers, text, and more.

Declaring Variables

To declare a variable in C#, you specify its data type followed by a name. Here are some common data types and variable declarations:

int age; *// Declares an integer variable named 'age'*

double price; *// Declares a double variable named 'price'*

string name; *// Declares a string variable named 'name'*

bool isStudent; *// Declares a boolean variable named 'isStudent'*

Initializing Variables

After declaring a variable, you can assign a value to it using the assignment operator (=). This is known as initialization. Here's how you initialize variables:

age = 30; *// Initializes 'age' with the value 30*

price = 19.99; *// Initializes 'price' with the value 19.99*

name = "John"; *// Initializes 'name' with the string "John"*

isStudent = **true**; *// Initializes 'isStudent' with the boolean value 'true'*

You can also declare and initialize variables in a single line:

int age = 30; *// Declares and initializes 'age'*

double price = 19.99; *// Declares and initializes 'price'*

string name = "John"; *// Declares and initializes 'name'*

bool isStudent = **true**; *// Declares and initializes 'isStudent'*

Data Types

C# provides various data types for storing different kinds of data. Here are some common data types:

- **Numeric Types**:

– int: Represents 32-bit signed integers.

– double: Represents double-precision floating-point numbers.

– float: Represents single-precision floating-point numbers.

– decimal: Represents decimal numbers with high precision.

- **Text Types**:

– string: Represents a sequence of characters (text).

– char: Represents a single character.

- **Boolean Type**:

– bool: Represents a Boolean value, either true or false.

- **Other Types**:

– DateTime: Represents dates and times.

– enum: Represents a set of named constants.

Type Inference (var keyword)

In C#, you can use the var keyword to declare variables without specifying the data type explicitly. The compiler infers the data type based on the assigned value:

var age = 30; *// 'age' is inferred as an int*

var price = 19.99; *// 'price' is inferred as a double*

var name = "John"; *// 'name' is inferred as a string*

var isStudent = **true**; *// 'isStudent' is inferred as a bool*

While var can make your code more concise, it's essential to use it judiciously to maintain code clarity and readability.

Constants

In addition to variables, you can declare constants in C# using the const keyword. Constants have a fixed value that cannot be changed once defined:

const double pi = 3.14159; *// Declares a constant 'pi'*

Constants are useful when you have values in your program that should not change during its execution.

Understanding variables and data types is a crucial first step in C# programming. They provide the foundation for storing and manipulating data in your applications. In the next sections, we'll explore how to work with these variables and data types more effectively through expressions, operations, and control flow.

Section 2.3: Input and Output in C

In this section, we'll explore how to perform input and output operations in C#. Input allows your program to receive data from external sources like users, files, or other programs, while output enables your program to communicate results or information.

Console Input

C# provides several methods for reading user input from the console. One of the most common methods is Console.ReadLine(), which reads a line of text entered by the user and returns it as a string:

Console.Write("Enter your name: ");

string name = Console.ReadLine();

Console.WriteLine($"Hello, {name}!");

In this code: - Console.Write("Enter your name: "); displays a prompt to the user. - Console.ReadLine(); waits for the user to input text and stores it in the name variable. - Console.WriteLine($"Hello, {name}!"); prints a greeting using the entered name.

You can use similar methods to read other types of data like numbers or characters and convert them to appropriate data types.

Console Output

We've already seen Console.WriteLine() for output, which writes text followed by a newline character. You can also use Console.Write() to output text without a newline:

Console.Write("Hello, ");

Console.Write("World!");

This code outputs "Hello, World!" on a single line.

String Interpolation

String interpolation is a convenient way to embed expressions within strings. You can use the $ symbol followed by {} to include variable values or expressions in a string:

```
string name = "Alice";

int age = 25;

Console.WriteLine($"Hello, {name}! You are {age} years old.");
```

String interpolation makes it easy to create dynamic and readable messages.

Formatting Output

You can format output using various format specifiers. For example, to format a number with a specific number of decimal places, use the F specifier:

```
double price = 19.99;

Console.WriteLine($"Price: {price:F2}");
```

This code outputs the price with two decimal places: "Price: 19.99."

Console Input Conversion

When reading input from the console, you may need to convert it to the appropriate data type. For example, to read an integer, you can use int.Parse():

```
Console.Write("Enter your age: ");
```

```
string ageInput = Console.ReadLine();

int age = int.Parse(ageInput);
```

However, be cautious when using conversion methods like Parse() as they can throw exceptions if the input cannot be converted.

Error Handling

To handle potential conversion errors, you can use int.TryParse() and similar methods. These methods attempt to parse the input and return a Boolean indicating success:

```
Console.Write("Enter your age: ");

string ageInput = Console.ReadLine();

if (int.TryParse(ageInput, out int age))

{

Console.WriteLine($"You entered a valid age: {age}");

}

else

{

Console.WriteLine("Invalid input. Please enter a valid age.");

}
```

This code checks if the input can be parsed as an integer and handles both valid and invalid cases gracefully.

File Input and Output

In addition to console input and output, C# allows you to work with files. You can read data from files using classes like File and StreamReader, and write data to files using classes like File and StreamWriter. File operations are essential when working with larger datasets or when you need to save and retrieve data between program runs.

Understanding input and output operations is crucial as they enable your programs to interact with users, external data, and other software components. In the next sections, we'll explore more advanced topics, including control flow, decision making, and loops, which are essential for building complex C# applications.

Section 2.4: Control Flow and Decision Making

Control flow and decision-making are fundamental concepts in programming. They allow your C# programs to make choices, repeat actions, and follow specific paths based on conditions. In this section, we'll explore control flow structures like conditional statements and loops.

Conditional Statements (if, else, and switch)

Conditional statements are used to make decisions in your program. C# provides several conditional constructs, with the most common being if, else if, else, and switch.

The if Statement

The if statement allows you to execute a block of code if a condition is true. Here's a basic example:

```
int age = 25;

if (age >= 18)

{

Console.WriteLine("You are an adult.");

}
```

In this code, if the condition age >= 18 is true, the message "You are an adult" will be displayed.

The else Statement

You can use the else statement to provide an alternative block of code to execute when the if condition is false:

```
int age = 15;

if (age >= 18)

{

Console.WriteLine("You are an adult.");

}

else

{

Console.WriteLine("You are not yet an adult.");

}
```

Here, since age is 15 and does not meet the age >= 18 condition, the message "You are not yet an adult" will be displayed.

The else if Statement

You can use the else if statement to check additional conditions if the previous if condition is false:

```
int score = 85;

if (score >= 90)

{

Console.WriteLine("Excellent!");

}

else if (score >= 70)

{

Console.WriteLine("Good!");

}

else

{

Console.WriteLine("Needs improvement.");

}
```

In this code, the program checks multiple conditions and prints different messages based on the score.

The switch Statement

The switch statement allows you to perform different actions based on the value of an expression:

```
int day = 3;

string dayName;

switch (day)

{

case 1:

dayName = "Monday";

break;

case 2:

dayName = "Tuesday";

break;

case 3:

dayName = "Wednesday";

break;

default:

dayName = "Unknown";

break;

}

Console.WriteLine($"Today is {dayName}");
```

Here, the switch statement assigns a day name based on the value of day. In this case, “Wednesday” will be assigned to dayName.

Loops (for, while, do-while, and foreach)

Loops are used to repeat a block of code multiple times. C# provides several loop constructs to cater to different scenarios.

The for Loop

The for loop allows you to execute a block of code a specific number of times. It consists of an initialization, a condition, and an iteration expression:

```
for (int i = 1; i <= 5; i++)

{

Console.WriteLine($"Iteration {i}");

}
```

This for loop prints "Iteration 1" to "Iteration 5" to the console.

The while Loop

The while loop repeatedly executes a block of code as long as a specified condition is true:

```
int count = 0;

while (count < 5)

{

Console.WriteLine($"Count: {count}");

count++;

}
```

This while loop prints "Count: 0" to "Count: 4" to the console.

The do-while Loop

The do-while loop is similar to the while loop, but it guarantees that the code block is executed at least once, even if the condition is initially false:

```
int n = 5;
do
{
Console.WriteLine($"Iteration {n}");
n++;
} while (n < 5);
```

In this example, the code block is executed once before checking the condition, so "Iteration 5" is printed.

The foreach Loop

The foreach loop is used for iterating over collections like arrays or lists. It simplifies the process of iterating through elements:

```
int[] numbers = { 1, 2, 3, 4, 5 };
foreach (int num in numbers)
{
Console.WriteLine($"Number: {num}");
}
```

This foreach loop iterates through the numbers array and prints each number to the console.

Control flow and decision-making are vital for building dynamic and interactive C# programs. By using conditional statements and loops effectively, you can create programs that respond to different situations and perform repetitive tasks. In the following sections, we'll delve deeper into more advanced C# concepts, allowing you to build even more sophisticated applications.

Section 2.5: Debugging and Error Handling

Debugging and error handling are critical aspects of software development. In this section, we'll explore techniques for identifying and fixing issues in your C# code and handling errors gracefully.

Debugging Your Code

Debugging is the process of finding and fixing errors (bugs) in your code. C# development environments like Visual Studio offer powerful debugging tools to assist you in this process.

Setting Breakpoints

One of the most common debugging techniques is setting breakpoints in your code. A breakpoint is a point where the program execution temporarily stops, allowing you to inspect variables, step through code, and identify issues.

To set a breakpoint in Visual Studio, click in the margin next to the line of code where you want to pause execution. A red dot will appear, indicating the breakpoint. When you run your program in debug mode, it will stop at the breakpoint.

Stepping Through Code

Once your program is paused at a breakpoint, you can step through your code one line at a time. Visual Studio provides options like "Step Into" (F11) to go into method calls, "Step Over" (F10) to execute the current line without diving into method calls, and "Step Out" (Shift+F11) to return from a method call.

These options help you navigate your code and understand how it executes, making it easier to spot errors.

Inspecting Variables

While debugging, you can inspect the values of variables and expressions. In Visual Studio, you can hover over a variable to see its current value or use the "Watch" window to monitor specific variables during debugging.

Debugging Tools

Visual Studio offers various debugging tools, such as the Immediate window for executing code during debugging, the Call Stack for tracing function calls, and the Locals window for viewing local variables.

Error Handling

In addition to debugging, it's essential to handle errors gracefully in your C# code. Errors can occur due to various reasons, such as invalid user input, file not found, or network issues. Handling errors ensures that your program doesn't crash and provides helpful feedback to users.

Exception Handling

C# uses exception handling to deal with runtime errors. You can use try, catch, finally, and throw blocks to manage exceptions.

```
try
{
// Code that may throw an exception
int result = 10 / int.Parse("0");
}
catch (DivideByZeroException)
{
Console.WriteLine("Division by zero error.");
}
catch (FormatException)
{
Console.WriteLine("Invalid input format.");
}
finally
{
Console.WriteLine("Cleanup code executed.");
}
```

In this example, if an exception occurs during the division operation or parsing, the appropriate catch block is executed, and then the finally block ensures that cleanup code is run, regardless of whether an exception occurred or not.

Custom Exceptions

You can create custom exception classes by deriving from the Exception class to handle specific application-specific errors. Custom exceptions should provide meaningful information about the error and how to resolve it.

Logging

Logging is another crucial aspect of error handling. You can use logging libraries like Serilog or NLog to record information about errors and events in your application. Logging helps you diagnose issues in production environments and monitor application health.

```
using Serilog;

Log.Logger = new LoggerConfiguration()

.WriteTo.Console()

.WriteTo.File("log.txt")

.CreateLogger();

try

{

// Code that may throw an exception

}
```

```
catch (Exception ex)
{
Log.Error(ex, "An error occurred.");
}
finally
{
Log.CloseAndFlush();
}
```

This example demonstrates using Serilog to log errors and messages to both the console and a log file.

Testing

Testing is an essential part of error prevention. Writing unit tests using frameworks like NUnit or xUnit helps identify issues early in the development process. Automated tests ensure that your code behaves as expected and catches regressions when making changes.

By mastering debugging techniques and implementing robust error handling strategies, you can build more reliable and maintainable C# applications. These skills are essential as you progress in your C# development journey and work on larger and more complex projects.

Chapter 3: Object-Oriented Programming (OOP) Fundamentals

Section 3.1: Understanding Classes and Objects

In this section, we'll dive into the fundamental concepts of Object-Oriented Programming (OOP). OOP is a programming paradigm that revolves around the concept of objects, which represent real-world entities and their interactions. Understanding classes and objects is at the core of OOP in C#.

What is Object-Oriented Programming (OOP)?

Object-Oriented Programming is a programming paradigm that structures code around objects, which are instances of classes. Objects encapsulate data (attributes or properties) and behavior (methods or functions) into a single unit. OOP promotes concepts like encapsulation, inheritance, and polymorphism, making code more modular, reusable, and easier to maintain.

Classes and Objects

In OOP, a class is a blueprint or template for creating objects. It defines the structure and behavior that objects of that class will have. A class encapsulates data (attributes) and methods (functions) that operate on that data.

Here's a simple example of a class in C#:

```
public class Person

{
```

```
// Properties (attributes)

public string Name { get; set; }

public int Age { get; set; }

// Methods (behavior)

public void SayHello()

{

Console.WriteLine($"Hello, my name is {Name} and I'm {Age} years old.");

}

}
```

In this code: - We define a Person class with two properties: Name and Age. - The SayHello method is a behavior associated with the Person class, allowing a Person object to introduce itself.

To create an object of the Person class, you use the new keyword:

```
Person person1 = new Person();

person1.Name = "Alice";

person1.Age = 30;

person1.SayHello(); // Outputs: Hello, my name is Alice and I'm 30 years old.
```

Here, person1 is an instance of the Person class, and you can access its properties and methods.

Encapsulation

Encapsulation is the concept of bundling data and methods that operate on that data into a single unit (a class). It helps hide the internal details of how an object works, exposing only what's necessary. In our Person class, the properties Name and Age are encapsulated within the class, and external code can access them using getters and setters.

Constructors

Constructors are special methods that are used to initialize objects when they are created. They have the same name as the class and are called when you use the new keyword to create an object. Here's an example constructor for the Person class:

```
public class Person

{

public string Name { get; set; }

public int Age { get; set; }

// Constructor

public Person(string name, int age)

{

Name = name;

Age = age;

}

//...
```

}

You can create a Person object with this constructor:

Person person2 = **new** Person("Bob", 25);

Object Initialization Syntax

C# provides object initialization syntax, allowing you to create and initialize objects concisely:

Person person3 = **new** Person

{

Name = "Charlie",

Age = 40

};

This syntax is especially useful when you want to set several properties during object creation.

Understanding classes and objects is the foundation of OOP in C#. Classes define the blueprint for objects, and objects are instances of these classes that encapsulate data and behavior. In the next sections, we'll explore advanced OOP concepts like inheritance, polymorphism, and abstraction, which enable you to build complex and flexible C# applications.

Section 3.2: Encapsulation and Access Modifiers

In this section, we'll delve into the concept of encapsulation and explore access modifiers in C#. Encapsulation is a fundamental principle of Object-Oriented Programming (OOP) that allows you to control access to the internal state and behavior of objects. Access modifiers help define the visibility and accessibility of members (fields, properties, methods, etc.) within a class.

Encapsulation in OOP

Encapsulation is the bundling of data (attributes or properties) and the methods (functions or behavior) that operate on that data into a single unit called a class. It provides several benefits, including:

- **Data Hiding**: Encapsulation hides the internal details of a class from external code. This means that the internal representation of an object can change without affecting the code that uses the object.

- **Controlled Access**: It allows you to define which members of a class are accessible from outside and which are not. This control prevents unauthorized modifications or access to sensitive data.

- **Code Reusability**: Encapsulated classes can be easily reused in different parts of the code or in other projects, promoting code modularity.

Access Modifiers

Access modifiers in C# determine the visibility and accessibility of class members. There are several access modifiers available, including:

- **public**: Members marked as public are accessible from any part of the code, both within the class and externally.

- **private**: Members marked as private are only accessible within the same class. They are not visible or accessible from outside the class.

- **protected**: Members marked as protected are accessible within the class and by derived classes (classes that inherit from the base class).

- **internal**: Members marked as internal are accessible within the same assembly (a compiled unit of code, such as a DLL or executable).

- **protected internal**: Members marked as protected internal are accessible within the same assembly and by derived classes.

- **private protected**: Members marked as private protected are accessible within the same assembly and by derived classes, but only if they are in the same assembly.

Example of Encapsulation and Access Modifiers

Let's consider an example using a BankAccount class:

```
public class BankAccount

{

// Private fields (encapsulated data)

private string accountNumber;

private decimal balance;

// Constructor
```

```
public BankAccount(string accountNumber)

{

this.accountNumber = accountNumber;

this.balance = 0.0m;

}

// Public method (encapsulated behavior)

public void Deposit(decimal amount)

{

if (amount > 0)

{

balance += amount;

}

}

// Public method (encapsulated behavior)

public bool Withdraw(decimal amount)

{

if (amount > 0 && balance >= amount)

{

balance -= amount;

return true;
```

```
}
return false;
}
// Public property (encapsulated data with access control)
public decimal Balance
{
get { return balance; }
}
}
```

In this BankAccount class: - accountNumber and balance are private fields, encapsulating data and hiding it from external code. - Deposit and Withdraw are public methods that provide controlled access to the account's behavior. - Balance is a public property that allows external code to read the account's balance but not modify it directly.

By using encapsulation and access modifiers, you can create classes that provide a clear interface to their functionality while keeping their internal details hidden and controlled. This promotes code maintainability, flexibility, and security.

Section 3.3: Inheritance and Polymorphism

Inheritance and polymorphism are key concepts in Object-Oriented Programming (OOP) that enable code reuse, flexibility, and extensibility. In this section, we'll explore these concepts and how they are implemented in C#.

Inheritance

Inheritance is a mechanism in which a new class (derived or child class) is created by inheriting properties and behaviors (fields and methods) from an existing class (base or parent class). The derived class can extend or override the functionality of the base class.

Creating a Derived Class

To create a derived class in C#, you use the : symbol followed by the base class name in the class declaration. Here's an example:

```
public class Animal
{
public void Eat()
{
Console.WriteLine("Animal is eating.");
}
}
public class Dog : Animal
{
public void Bark()
{
Console.WriteLine("Dog is barking.");
}
```

```
}
```

In this example, the Dog class is derived from the Animal class. It inherits the Eat method from Animal and adds its own method, Bark.

Overriding Base Class Members

Derived classes can override base class members to provide their own implementation. To do this, you use the override keyword. Here's an example with an overridden method:

```
public class Shape
{
public virtual void Draw()
{
Console.WriteLine("Drawing a shape.");
}
}
public class Circle : Shape
{
public override void Draw()
{
Console.WriteLine("Drawing a circle.");
}
```

```
}
```

In this example, the Circle class overrides the Draw method of the Shape class to provide its own implementation.

Polymorphism

Polymorphism is the ability of objects of different classes to be treated as objects of a common base class. It allows you to write code that works with objects at a higher level of abstraction, regardless of their specific derived types.

Using Polymorphism

To leverage polymorphism in C#, you can declare variables and parameters of the base class type and assign objects of derived classes to them. Here's an example:

```
Shape shape1 = new Circle();

shape1.Draw(); // Calls the overridden Draw method in Circle class
```

In this example, the shape1 variable is of type Shape, but it refers to an instance of the Circle class. When you call shape1.Draw(), it calls the Draw method from the Circle class, demonstrating polymorphism.

Virtual and Override Keywords

To enable polymorphism, you use the virtual keyword in the base class for methods that can be overridden. In the derived class, you use the override keyword to indicate that you're providing a specific implementation for that method.

```
public class Shape
```

```
{
public virtual void Draw()
{
Console.WriteLine("Drawing a shape.");
}
}
public class Circle : Shape
{
public override void Draw()
{
Console.WriteLine("Drawing a circle.");
}
}
```

The virtual keyword allows derived classes to override the method, and the override keyword specifies the overridden method in the derived class.

Abstract Classes and Methods

C# also supports abstract classes and methods, which are used when you want to create a base class with certain methods that must be implemented by derived classes. Abstract classes cannot be instantiated; they are meant to be extended by other classes.

```
public abstract class Shape
```

```
{
public abstract void Draw(); // Abstract method, must be implemented by derived classes
}
```

In this example, Shape is an abstract class with an abstract method Draw. Any class that derives from Shape must provide an implementation for Draw.

Inheritance and polymorphism are powerful mechanisms for code reuse and building flexible and extensible software. By using these concepts, you can create hierarchies of classes that model real-world relationships and behaviors effectively. In the following sections, we'll explore more advanced OOP concepts like interfaces and abstraction in C#.

Section 3.4: Abstraction and Interfaces

Abstraction and interfaces are essential concepts in Object-Oriented Programming (OOP) that promote code flexibility, modularity, and maintainability. In this section, we'll explore these concepts and their implementation in C#.

Abstraction

Abstraction is the process of simplifying complex systems by modeling classes based on their essential properties and behaviors while hiding unnecessary details. Abstraction allows you to focus on what an object does rather than how it does it.

Abstract Classes

In C#, you can create abstract classes that serve as a blueprint for other classes but cannot be instantiated themselves. Abstract classes may contain both abstract and non-abstract (concrete) members (methods, properties, fields). Classes derived from an abstract class must implement all its abstract members.

```
public abstract class Shape

{

public abstract void Draw(); // Abstract method, must be implemented by derived classes

public void Move(int x, int y)

{

// Concrete method

Console.WriteLine($"Moving to ({x}, {y})");

}

}
```

In this example, Shape is an abstract class with an abstract method Draw and a concrete method Move.

Abstract Methods

Abstract methods in an abstract class have no implementation in the base class and are marked with the abstract keyword. Derived classes must provide an implementation for these methods.

```
public abstract class Shape
{
public abstract void Draw();
}
```

Derived classes like Circle and Rectangle must implement the Draw method.

Interfaces

Interfaces define a contract of methods, properties, events, or indexers that implementing classes must adhere to. Unlike abstract classes, a class can implement multiple interfaces, promoting code reuse and flexibility.

Creating Interfaces

In C#, you define an interface using the interface keyword. Interfaces consist of method signatures and property declarations without implementations.

```
public interface IDrawable
{
void Draw(); // Method signature
int Width { get; } // Property declaration
}
```

In this example, IDrawable is an interface with a Draw method and a read-only Width property.

Implementing Interfaces

A class can implement an interface by providing concrete implementations for all the members defined in the interface.

```
public class Circle : IDrawable

{

public void Draw()

{

Console.WriteLine("Drawing a circle.");

}

public int Width

{

get { return 10; }

}

}
```

In this example, the Circle class implements the IDrawable interface, providing its own implementation for the Draw method and the Width property.

Using Interfaces for Polymorphism

Interfaces enable polymorphism, allowing you to work with objects of different classes that implement the same interface using a common interface reference.

```
IDrawable shape1 = new Circle();

IDrawable shape2 = new Rectangle();

shape1.Draw(); // Calls the Draw method of Circle

shape2.Draw(); // Calls the Draw method of Rectangle
```

In this example, shape1 and shape2 are of type IDrawable, but they refer to instances of different classes that implement the interface. Polymorphism enables you to treat these objects uniformly.

Benefits of Abstraction and Interfaces

Abstraction and interfaces play a crucial role in OOP by allowing you to:

- Define contracts and standardize behavior for classes.
- Achieve code reusability through inheritance and interface implementation.
- Work with objects at a higher level of abstraction, promoting flexibility.
- Separate concerns and reduce code complexity by modeling only essential properties and behaviors.

By mastering abstraction and interfaces in C#, you can design more flexible and maintainable software systems that can easily adapt to changing requirements and scale with your application's growth.

Section 3.5: Working with Exception Handling in OOP

Exception handling is a critical aspect of Object-Oriented Programming (OOP) that allows you to handle runtime errors gracefully. In this section, we'll explore how exception handling works in OOP using C#.

Exception Handling Basics

Exception handling is the process of responding to and managing unexpected runtime errors or exceptional situations that may occur during program execution. These errors can be due to various reasons, such as invalid user input, file not found, or network issues.

In C#, exception handling is facilitated through keywords like try, catch, finally, and throw.

The try and catch Blocks

The try block is used to enclose code that might throw an exception. If an exception occurs within the try block, the program immediately jumps to the appropriate catch block, which handles the exception.

```
try
{
// Code that may throw an exception
}
catch (Exception ex)
{
```

```
// Handle the exception
Console.WriteLine($"An error occurred: {ex.Message}");
}
```

In this example, if an exception occurs within the try block, it's caught by the catch block, and you can handle it by displaying an error message.

The finally Block

The finally block is used to specify code that should be executed regardless of whether an exception occurred or not. It's often used for cleanup operations.

```
try
{
// Code that may throw an exception
}
catch (Exception ex)
{
// Handle the exception
Console.WriteLine($"An error occurred: {ex.Message}");
}
finally
{
```

```
// Cleanup code
Console.WriteLine("Cleanup");
}
```

In this example, the finally block ensures that the cleanup code is executed, even if an exception is thrown.

Exception Classes

In C#, exceptions are represented as objects of classes derived from the System.Exception class. The .NET Framework provides a hierarchy of exception classes that cover various types of exceptions.

- System.Exception: The base class for all exceptions.
- System.SystemException: The base class for system-related exceptions.
- System.ApplicationException: The base class for exceptions generated by application code.

You can also create custom exception classes by deriving from these base classes to handle specific errors in your application.

```
public class CustomException : ApplicationException
{
public CustomException(string message) : base(message)
{
}
}
```

Throwing Exceptions

You can use the throw statement to throw an exception explicitly. This is useful when you want to signal an exceptional condition in your code.

```
public int Divide(int dividend, int divisor)

{

if (divisor == 0)

{

throw new DivideByZeroException("Division by zero is not allowed.");

}

return dividend / divisor;

}
```

In this example, the Divide method throws a DivideByZeroException if the divisor is zero.

Custom Exception Handling

Handling exceptions in OOP allows you to create custom error-handling strategies. You can catch specific types of exceptions, log errors, and provide meaningful feedback to users. This helps in making your applications robust and user-friendly.

```
try

{

int result = Divide(10, 0);
```

```
Console.WriteLine($"Result: {result}");
}
catch (DivideByZeroException ex)
{
Console.WriteLine($"Division error: {ex.Message}");
}
catch (CustomException ex)
{
Console.WriteLine($"Custom error: {ex.Message}");
}
```

In this example, we catch specific exceptions and provide custom error messages for each type of exception.

Exception handling is a fundamental aspect of OOP that ensures your programs can gracefully recover from unexpected errors. It's essential to handle exceptions appropriately to create reliable and user-friendly applications. By mastering exception handling techniques, you can improve the robustness and reliability of your C# applications.

Chapter 4: Advanced OOP Concepts

Section 4.1: Generics and Generic Collections

In this section, we'll explore one of the advanced Object-Oriented Programming (OOP) concepts in C#: Generics. Generics allow you to create classes, methods, and interfaces that work with different data types while providing type safety. We'll focus on generics and their application in creating generic collections.

Introduction to Generics

Generics enable you to write code that can work with a variety of data types while maintaining compile-time type safety. They allow you to define classes, methods, or interfaces with placeholder types (type parameters) that are specified at the time of use. This flexibility is particularly valuable when working with collections, algorithms, and data structures that need to accommodate different types of data.

Generic Classes

A generic class is a class that can work with different data types. You define a generic class by specifying one or more type parameters enclosed in angle brackets (<>) when declaring the class.

```
public class GenericList<T>

{

private T[] items;

public GenericList(int size)
```

```
{
items = new T[size];
}
public void Add(int index, T item)
{
items[index] = item;
}
public T Get(int index)
{
return items[index];
}
}
```

In this example, GenericList<T> is a generic class that can store elements of any type T. The T type parameter is a placeholder for the actual data type that will be used when creating an instance of the class.

Using Generic Classes

To use a generic class, you specify the actual data type when creating an instance of the class. This is called providing type arguments.

```
GenericList<int> intList = new GenericList<int>(5);
intList.Add(0, 42);
int value = intList.Get(0); // value is 42
```

```
GenericList<string> stringList = new GenericList<string>(3);

stringList.Add(0, "Hello");

string text = stringList.Get(0); // text is "Hello"
```

In this code, we create two instances of GenericList, one to store integers and the other to store strings. The type arguments (int and string) specify the actual data types.

Generic Methods

Generics can also be applied to methods. A generic method can work with different data types, and you define type parameters for the method similarly to generic classes.

```
public class Utilities

{

public T Max<T>(T a, T b) where T : IComparable<T>

{

return a.CompareTo(b) > 0 ? a : b;

}

}
```

In this example, the Max method is generic and can determine the maximum value of any type T that implements the IComparable<T> interface.

Generic Constraints

You can impose constraints on type parameters using the where keyword. Constraints specify that the type argument must implement certain interfaces, derive from a specific class, or have a default constructor.

```
public class ExampleClass<T> where T : IComparable<T>
{
//...
}
```

In this code, T must implement the IComparable<T> interface.

Generic Collections

C# provides a set of generic collection classes in the System.Collections.Generic namespace, such as List<T>, Dictionary<TKey, TValue>, and Queue<T>. These collections offer type-safe storage for various data types and are widely used in C# programming.

```
List<int> numbers = new List<int>();

numbers.Add(42);

int firstNumber = numbers[0]; //firstNumber is 42

Dictionary<string, double> grades = new Dictionary<string, double>();

grades["Alice"] = 95.5;

double aliceGrade = grades["Alice"]; // aliceGrade is 95.5
```

In this example, we use the generic List<T> and Dictionary<TKey, TValue> to store integers and key-value pairs, respectively.

Generics are a powerful feature in C# that allows you to write flexible and type-safe code that can work with different data types. They are especially useful when working with collections and algorithms where type flexibility is required. In the following sections, we'll explore more advanced OOP concepts, including delegates, events, and lambda expressions.

Section 4.2: Delegates and Events

Delegates and events are powerful mechanisms in C# that enable you to work with functions as first-class objects and implement event-driven programming. In this section, we'll explore these concepts and their applications.

Delegates

A delegate is a reference type that can represent a reference to a method with a particular parameter list and return type. Delegates allow you to treat methods as first-class citizens, making it possible to pass methods as arguments to other methods, store them in data structures, and invoke them dynamically at runtime.

Defining Delegates

To define a delegate, you specify its signature, which includes the return type and parameters of the method it can reference.

```
public delegate void MyDelegate(int x, int y);
```

In this example, MyDelegate is a delegate type that can reference methods with two int parameters and no return value (void).

Using Delegates

You can create instances of delegates and assign them methods that match their signature. Then, you can invoke the delegate to execute the referenced method.

```
public void Add(int a, int b)
{
Console.WriteLine($"Sum: {a + b}");
}
MyDelegate addDelegate = Add;
addDelegate(5, 7); // Calls the Add method
```

In this code, addDelegate references the Add method and can be invoked to execute Add.

Multicast Delegates

Delegates can also be combined to create multicast delegates that reference multiple methods. When a multicast delegate is invoked, it calls all the referenced methods in the order they were added.

```
public void Method1() { Console.WriteLine("Method 1"); }
public void Method2() { Console.WriteLine("Method 2"); }
MyDelegate multicastDelegate = Method1;
multicastDelegate += Method2;
multicastDelegate(); // Calls Method1 and Method2
```

In this example, multicastDelegate references both Method1 and Method2, so invoking it calls both methods.

Events

Events are a higher-level abstraction built on top of delegates and are commonly used in event-driven programming. They allow objects to notify other objects that something of interest has occurred.

Declaring Events

To declare an event, you define an event handler delegate type and create an event based on that delegate type.

```
public delegate void EventHandler(object sender, EventArgs e);

public class Button

{

public event EventHandler Click;

public void SimulateClick()

{

Click?.Invoke(this, EventArgs.Empty);

}

}
```

In this example, Button declares a Click event using the EventHandler delegate type.

Subscribing to Events

To subscribe to an event and handle it, you add an event handler method to the event using the += operator.

```
Button button = new Button();

button.Click += ButtonClickHandler;

void ButtonClickHandler(object sender, EventArgs e)

{

Console.WriteLine("Button clicked!");

}
```

In this code, the ButtonClickHandler method is subscribed to the Click event of the button object.

Raising Events

To raise (invoke) an event, you call it like a method. Before invoking an event, it's a good practice to check if it's not null using the null-conditional operator (?.) to avoid null reference exceptions.

```
button.SimulateClick(); // Raises the Click event
```

In this example, calling SimulateClick on the button object raises the Click event.

Event Handlers and Event Args

Event handlers are methods that are invoked when an event occurs. They must have a specific signature matching the delegate type associated with the event. Event arguments (often derived from EventArgs) can provide additional information about the event.

```
public class MyEventArgs : EventArgs
{
public string Message { get; set; }
}
public class MyEventPublisher
{
public event EventHandler<MyEventArgs> MyEventOccurred;
public void RaiseEvent(string message)
{
var args = new MyEventArgs { Message = message };
MyEventOccurred?.Invoke(this, args);
}
}
```

In this example, MyEventPublisher raises an event with custom event arguments (MyEventArgs).

Delegates and events are fundamental to implementing event-driven and callback-based programming in C#. They enable decoupling of components and the creation of extensible and flexible software. By understanding these concepts, you can build responsive and event-driven applications with ease.

Section 4.3: Lambda Expressions and LINQ

Lambda expressions and LINQ (Language-Integrated Query) are powerful features in C# that simplify working with collections and provide concise syntax for writing queries and transformations. In this section, we'll delve into these features and how they enhance your coding experience.

Lambda Expressions

Lambda expressions are anonymous functions that allow you to write inline, concise, and readable code for simple operations. They are particularly useful when you need to pass functions as arguments or return functions from other functions.

Syntax

A lambda expression has the following syntax:

```
(parameters) => expression
```

Lambda expressions can have zero or more parameters and a single expression. If there are no parameters, you use empty parentheses.

Example

```
// Traditional method

int Square(int x)

{

return x * x;

}
```

// Equivalent lambda expression

Func<int, int> square = x => x * x;

In this example, square is a lambda expression that calculates the square of a number.

LINQ (Language-Integrated Query)

LINQ is a set of language features that allow you to perform queries on collections of objects, databases, XML, and more using a uniform syntax. LINQ simplifies querying and transforming data by providing a fluent, SQL-like syntax directly in C# code.

Query Operators

LINQ offers a set of query operators (methods) that operate on sequences, such as Where, Select, OrderBy, and GroupBy, to filter, project, order, and group data.

var numbers = **new** List<int> { 1, 2, 3, 4, 5 };

var evenNumbers = numbers.Where(x => x % 2 == 0); *// Filters even numbers*

var squaredNumbers = numbers.Select(x => x * x); *// Squares each number*

In this code, Where and Select are LINQ query operators used to filter and transform the numbers collection, respectively.

Method Syntax vs. Query Syntax

LINQ provides two syntaxes: method syntax (using extension methods) and query syntax (using SQL-like keywords). Both are functionally equivalent, and you can choose the one that suits your coding style.

Method Syntax

```
var evenNumbers = numbers.Where(x => x % 2 == 0).ToList();
```

Query Syntax

```
var evenNumbers = (from num in numbers where num % 2 == 0
select num).ToList();
```

LINQ to Objects

LINQ can be used to query in-memory collections like arrays, lists, and dictionaries. It also supports querying XML documents, databases, and other data sources.

```
var books = new List<Book>

{

new Book { Title = "C# in Depth", Author = "Jon Skeet" },

new Book { Title = "Clean Code", Author = "Robert C. Martin" },

// ...

};

var query = from book in books

where book.Author == "Jon Skeet"

select book.Title;
```

In this example, we use LINQ to query a collection of Book objects and select the titles of books authored by "Jon Skeet."

Benefits of Lambda Expressions and LINQ

Lambda expressions and LINQ offer several benefits:

- **Conciseness**: They allow you to write shorter and more readable code, reducing boilerplate.
- **Flexibility**: Lambda expressions enable the creation of inline functions, making code more flexible.
- **Expressiveness**: LINQ provides a readable and consistent way to query and transform data in various sources.
- **Type Safety**: Errors can be caught at compile time, reducing runtime exceptions.

By mastering lambda expressions and LINQ, you can write more expressive and efficient code for querying and manipulating data, leading to improved productivity and code maintainability.

Section 4.4: Design Patterns in C

Design patterns are proven solutions to common software design problems. They provide reusable and structured approaches to solving specific problems, improving code maintainability and scalability. In this section, we'll explore some of the commonly used design patterns in C#.

Creational Design Patterns

Singleton Pattern

The Singleton pattern ensures that a class has only one instance and provides a global point of access to that instance.

```
public sealed class Singleton
{
private static readonly Singleton instance = new Singleton();
private Singleton() { }
public static Singleton Instance => instance;
}
```

In this example, the Singleton class guarantees that only one instance is created and can be accessed through the Instance property.

Factory Pattern

The Factory pattern is used to create objects without specifying the exact class of object that will be created.

```
public interface IAnimal
{
void Speak();
}
public class Dog : IAnimal
```

```
{
public void Speak() => Console.WriteLine("Woof!");
}
public class Cat : IAnimal
{
public void Speak() => Console.WriteLine("Meow!");
}
public class AnimalFactory
{
public IAnimal CreateAnimal(string animalType)
{
return animalType switch
{
"Dog" => new Dog(),
"Cat" => new Cat(),
_ => throw new ArgumentException("Invalid animal type"),
};
}
}
```

In this example, the AnimalFactory class creates instances of IAnimal without exposing the concrete classes Dog and Cat.

Structural Design Patterns

Adapter Pattern

The Adapter pattern allows the interface of an existing class to be used as another interface. It is often used to make existing classes work with others without modifying their source code.

```
public interface ITarget

{

void Request();

}

public class Adaptee

{

public void SpecificRequest() => Console.WriteLine("Adaptee's specific request");

}

public class Adapter : ITarget

{

private readonly Adaptee adaptee;

public Adapter(Adaptee adaptee) => this.adaptee = adaptee;

public void Request()

{

adaptee.SpecificRequest();
```

```
}

}
```

In this example, the Adapter class adapts the Adaptee class to the ITarget interface.

Composite Pattern

The Composite pattern allows you to compose objects into tree structures to represent part-whole hierarchies. It enables clients to treat individual objects and compositions of objects uniformly.

```
public abstract class Component

{

public abstract void Operation();

}

public class Leaf : Component

{

public override void Operation() => Console.WriteLine("Leaf operation");

}

public class Composite : Component

{

private readonly List<Component> children = new List<Component>();
```

```
public void Add(Component component) =>
children.Add(component);

public override void Operation()

{

Console.WriteLine("Composite operation");

foreach (var child in children)

{

child.Operation();

}

}

}
```

In this example, the Composite class can contain both Leaf and other Composite objects, allowing you to build complex structures.

Behavioral Design Patterns

Observer Pattern

The Observer pattern defines a one-to-many dependency between objects so that when one object changes state, all its dependents are notified and updated automatically.

```
using System;

using System.Collections.Generic;

public interface IObserver
```

```
{
void Update(string message);
}
public class ConcreteObserver : IObserver
{
private readonly string name;
public ConcreteObserver(string name)
{
this.name = name;
}
public void Update(string message)
{
Console.WriteLine($"{name} received message: {message}");
}
}
public class ConcreteSubject
{
private readonly List<IObserver> observers = new List<IObserver>();
public void Attach(IObserver observer)
{
```

```
observers.Add(observer);
}
public void Notify(string message)
{
foreach (var observer in observers)
{
observer.Update(message);
}
}
}
```

In this example, ConcreteSubject maintains a list of observers and notifies them when its state changes.

Strategy Pattern

The Strategy pattern defines a family of algorithms, encapsulates each one, and makes them interchangeable. It allows the algorithm to vary independently from the clients that use it.

```
public interface IStrategy
{
void Execute();
}
public class ConcreteStrategyA : IStrategy
```

```
{
public void Execute() => Console.WriteLine("Executing Strategy A");
}
public class ConcreteStrategyB : IStrategy
{
public void Execute() => Console.WriteLine("Executing Strategy B");
}
public class Context
{
private readonly IStrategy strategy;
public Context(IStrategy strategy)
{
this.strategy = strategy;
}
public void ExecuteStrategy()
{
strategy.Execute();
}
}
```

In this example, the Context class can be configured with different strategies, allowing it to execute different algorithms.

Design patterns in C# provide solutions to common design problems, making your code more maintainable, scalable, and flexible. By understanding and applying these patterns, you can improve your software design and development skills.

Section 4.5: Unit Testing and Test-Driven Development (TDD)

Unit testing and Test-Driven Development (TDD) are essential practices in modern software development. They help ensure code correctness, maintainability, and robustness. In this section, we'll delve into the concepts of unit testing and how TDD can be a valuable approach in C# development.

Unit Testing

What Is Unit Testing?

Unit testing is the practice of testing individual units or components of a software application in isolation to ensure they work as expected. A unit can be a single method, function, or class. Unit tests are automated and run frequently during development to catch bugs early.

Benefits of Unit Testing

Unit testing offers several advantages:

- **Bug Detection**: Unit tests help catch bugs and regressions early in the development process, reducing the cost of fixing issues later.

- **Documentation**: Tests serve as documentation, providing examples of how to use a component.

- **Refactoring Safety**: Unit tests give developers confidence to refactor code because they can quickly detect if any functionality breaks.

- **Improved Design**: Writing tests often leads to more modular and loosely coupled code, improving software design.

xUnit and NUnit

C# has popular unit testing frameworks like xUnit and NUnit. These frameworks provide the infrastructure for writing and running unit tests.

xUnit Example

```
public class Calculator

{

public int Add(int a, int b) => a + b;

}

public class CalculatorTests

{
```

```
[Fact]
public void Add_ReturnsCorrectResult()
{
// Arrange
var calculator = new Calculator();
// Act
int result = calculator.Add(3, 4);
// Assert
Assert.Equal(7, result);
}
}
```

In this example, we use xUnit to write a test for the Add method of the Calculator class. The [Fact] attribute indicates a test, and Assert is used for assertions.

Test-Driven Development (TDD)

What Is TDD?

TDD is a development approach where you write tests before writing the actual code. The TDD cycle typically consists of three steps: red, green, and refactor.

1. **Red**: Write a failing test for the functionality you want to implement.
2. **Green**: Write the minimum code necessary to make the

test pass.
3. **Refactor**: Refactor the code while keeping the tests green.

TDD Benefits

TDD offers numerous advantages:

- **Clarity**: Tests clarify requirements and expected behavior.

- **Safety Net**: Tests serve as a safety net, ensuring that changes don't break existing functionality.

- **Incremental Development**: TDD encourages incremental development, leading to more manageable and less complex code.

- **Reduced Debugging**: Debugging is reduced because issues are caught early by tests.

TDD Example

Let's follow the TDD process to implement a simple StringCalculator class that can add numbers separated by commas.

1. **Red**: Write a failing test.

```
[Fact]

public void Add_EmptyString_ReturnsZero()

{

// Arrange
```

```
var calculator = new StringCalculator();

// Act

int result = calculator.Add("");

// Assert

Assert.Equal(0, result);

}
```

1. **Green**: Write the minimum code to make the test pass.

```
public class StringCalculator

{

public int Add(string input)

{

return 0;

}

}
```

1. **Refactor**: Refactor the code if necessary.
2. Repeat the cycle for additional functionality.

TDD Tips

- Start with simple tests and gradually add complexity.
- Write tests for edge cases and boundary conditions.

- Refactor code to improve its design and readability while ensuring tests remain green.

Unit testing and TDD are integral to creating reliable and maintainable C# applications. By writing tests early in the development process and continuously verifying the correctness of your code, you can increase software quality and reduce the time and effort spent on debugging and maintenance.

Chapter 5: Windows Forms and GUI Applications

Section 5.1: Introduction to Windows Forms

Windows Forms (WinForms) is a graphical user interface (GUI) framework for creating Windows desktop applications in C#. It provides a set of controls and tools for building Windows applications with rich user interfaces. In this section, we'll introduce you to the fundamentals of Windows Forms and how to get started with creating GUI applications in C#.

What Are Windows Forms?

Windows Forms is a part of the .NET Framework and later .NET Core, and it allows you to create desktop applications for Windows operating systems. Unlike web applications, Windows Forms applications run locally on a user's machine, providing a more responsive and interactive user experience.

Key Concepts

Form

In Windows Forms, a form is a primary window or dialog box that serves as the main user interface of your application. Forms are created by inheriting from the System.Windows.Forms.Form class. They can host various controls like buttons, text boxes, labels, and more.

Controls

Controls are UI elements that you place on a form to enable user interaction. Windows Forms provides a wide range of controls, including buttons, text boxes, checkboxes, radio buttons, list boxes, and combo boxes. You can customize the appearance and behavior of controls to suit your application's needs.

Event-Driven Programming

Windows Forms applications are event-driven, meaning they respond to user interactions and system events. You write event handlers to define how your application should respond when a user clicks a button, enters text, or performs other actions. Event handlers are methods that execute in response to specific events, such as button clicks or mouse movements.

Creating a Windows Forms Application

To create a Windows Forms application in Visual Studio:

1. Open Visual Studio and select "Create a new project."
2. Choose "Windows Forms App (.NET Core)" or a similar template.
3. Visual Studio will generate a default form for you, which you can customize by adding controls and event handlers.

Simple Windows Forms Example

Here's a simple example of a Windows Forms application with a button that displays a message when clicked:

```
using System;
```

```
using System.Windows.Forms;

namespace MyWinFormsApp

{

public partial class MainForm : Form

{

public MainForm()

{

InitializeComponent();

}

private void button1_Click(object sender, EventArgs e)

{

MessageBox.Show("Hello, WinForms!");

}

}

}
```

In this example, we create a form with a button control. When the button is clicked, it triggers the button1_Click event handler, which displays a message box.

Windows Forms provides a powerful platform for creating desktop applications with graphical user interfaces in C#. It's widely used for building Windows-based business applications, utilities, and various other desktop software. In the following sections, we will explore more advanced topics related to Windows Forms application development.

Section 5.2: Designing User Interfaces with WinForms

Designing user interfaces (UI) is a critical aspect of Windows Forms (WinForms) application development. Creating intuitive and visually appealing UIs enhances the user experience. In this section, we'll explore how to design user interfaces with WinForms.

Visual Design in WinForms

WinForms provides a visual design environment within Visual Studio, allowing you to design your UI using drag-and-drop controls. Here's how to get started:

1. **Open the Form Designer**: In Visual Studio, open the form you want to design by double-clicking the form's design file (usually ending with .Designer.cs).
2. **Toolbox**: The Toolbox panel on the left side of Visual Studio contains a list of controls you can use in your UI. Simply drag controls from the Toolbox onto the form.
3. **Properties Window**: The Properties window allows you to customize properties of controls and forms. You can set properties such as the control's name, text, size, and color.
4. **Layout**: WinForms provides layout controls like TableLayoutPanel and FlowLayoutPanel to help organize your UI elements. These controls help maintain a consistent and responsive design.

Common WinForms Controls

WinForms offers a wide range of controls to create various UI elements. Some common controls include:

- **Button**: For triggering actions when clicked.
- **Label**: For displaying static text.
- **TextBox**: For accepting user input.
- **ComboBox**: For selecting items from a dropdown list.
- **ListBox**: For displaying a list of items.
- **CheckBox** and **RadioButton**: For binary choices.
- **DataGridView**: For displaying tabular data.
- **PictureBox**: For displaying images.
- **MenuStrip** and **ToolStrip**: For creating menu bars and toolbars.
- **TabControl**: For creating tabbed interfaces.

Event Handling in WinForms

To make your UI interactive, you need to handle events triggered by user actions. WinForms controls generate events like button clicks, text changes, and mouse movements. You can write event handlers to respond to these events.

```
private void button1_Click(object sender, EventArgs e)
{
// Code to execute when the button is clicked.
```

```
}
```

In the Visual Studio Form Designer, you can double-click a control to generate an event handler automatically.

Layout and Anchoring

Proper layout is essential for ensuring your UI elements are displayed correctly on different screen sizes and resolutions. WinForms provides layout controls like TableLayoutPanel and FlowLayoutPanel to help with this.

Additionally, the "Anchor" property of controls allows you to specify how a control should behave when its parent container is resized. You can anchor controls to the left, right, top, or bottom, ensuring they resize and reposition appropriately.

Localization and Accessibility

WinForms supports localization, making it possible to create applications in multiple languages. You can easily translate your application's user interface by providing localized resource files for each language.

To make your WinForms applications more accessible, use accessible names and descriptions for controls, and ensure proper keyboard navigation and focus handling.

Testing and Debugging

Thoroughly test your WinForms applications to ensure they work as intended. Visual Studio provides debugging tools for identifying and fixing issues in your code and UI.

Conclusion

Designing user interfaces with WinForms is a crucial skill in Windows desktop application development. By using the visual design tools, handling events, and paying attention to layout and accessibility, you can create polished and user-friendly applications that meet your users' needs. In the following sections, we will explore more advanced topics related to WinForms development, including data binding and event-driven programming.

Section 5.3: Handling Events and User Input

Handling events and user input is a fundamental aspect of Windows Forms (WinForms) application development. In this section, we'll explore how to handle various types of events and user interactions in your WinForms applications.

Event-Driven Programming

WinForms applications are event-driven, meaning they respond to events triggered by user actions or system events. Events can be generated by controls (e.g., button clicks, mouse movements) or by the system (e.g., form load, window resize). To handle events, you write event handler methods that define what should happen when a specific event occurs.

Event Handling in WinForms

Here's a step-by-step guide on how to handle events in a WinForms application:

1. **Select a Control**: First, select the control (e.g., button, textbox) you want to add an event handler for in the Visual Studio Form Designer.

2. **Open the Properties Window**: In the Properties window, click the "Events" button (usually denoted by a lightning bolt icon). This lists the available events for the selected control.
3. **Double-Click an Event**: To create an event handler for a specific event, double-click the event name in the Properties window. Visual Studio will generate an event handler method and open the code editor.
4. **Write the Event Handler**: In the generated event handler method, write the code that should execute when the event is triggered.

```
private void button1_Click(object sender, EventArgs e)

{

// Code to execute when the button is clicked.

}
```

Common User Interactions

Button Click Event

Button controls are commonly used to trigger actions when clicked. You can create a button click event handler to define what happens when the button is pressed.

```
private void button1_Click(object sender, EventArgs e)

{

// Code to execute when the button is clicked.

}
```

Textbox TextChanged Event

The TextChanged event of a textbox is fired when the text inside the textbox changes. This can be useful for real-time validation or responding to user input.

```
private void textBox1_TextChanged(object sender, EventArgs e)

{

// Code to execute when the textbox text changes.

}
```

Mouse Events

Controls like buttons and panels can trigger mouse events such as MouseEnter, MouseLeave, and MouseClick. You can use these events to enhance user interactions.

```
private void button1_MouseEnter(object sender, EventArgs e)

{

// Code to execute when the mouse enters the button.

}
```

Keyboard Events

WinForms also allows you to handle keyboard events such as KeyPress, KeyDown, and KeyUp. These events are useful for responding to keyboard input.

```
private void Form1_KeyPress(object sender, KeyPressEventArgs e)

{
```

```
// Code to execute when a key is pressed.
}
```

Event Handling Best Practices

- Keep event handler methods concise and focused on the specific event's functionality.
- Use meaningful names for controls and events to improve code readability.
- Comment your code to explain the purpose of complex event handlers.
- Ensure that event handlers gracefully handle unexpected input or conditions to avoid crashes or errors.

Handling events and user input effectively is essential for creating responsive and interactive WinForms applications. By understanding the event-driven programming model and the various types of events, you can design applications that provide a smooth and intuitive user experience. In the next sections, we will explore more advanced WinForms topics, including data binding and working with controls.

Section 5.4: Working with Controls and Components

In Windows Forms (WinForms) applications, controls and components are the building blocks that allow you to create user interfaces and add functionality to your forms. This section explores the concepts of controls and components in WinForms and how to work with them effectively.

Understanding Controls

Controls are UI elements that you place on a form to enable user interaction. WinForms provides a wide range of controls, each serving a specific purpose. Some common controls include:

- **Button**: For triggering actions when clicked.
- **Label**: For displaying static text.
- **TextBox**: For accepting user input.
- **ComboBox**: For selecting items from a dropdown list.
- **ListBox**: For displaying a list of items.
- **CheckBox** and **RadioButton**: For binary choices.
- **DataGridView**: For displaying tabular data.
- **PictureBox**: For displaying images.
- **MenuStrip** and **ToolStrip**: For creating menu bars and toolbars.
- **TabControl**: For creating tabbed interfaces.

Each control has properties that you can customize to define its appearance and behavior. For example, you can set a button's text, size, color, and event handlers.

Placing and Configuring Controls

To add controls to a form in the Visual Studio Form Designer:

1. Open the form in the designer.
2. Open the Toolbox panel, which contains a list of available

controls.
3. Drag a control from the Toolbox onto the form.

Once a control is placed on the form, you can select it to configure its properties in the Properties window. You can also adjust the control's position and size by clicking and dragging its handles.

Container Controls

Container controls are special controls that can host other controls. They help you manage the layout of controls on a form. Common container controls include:

- **Panel**: A container for grouping and organizing controls.
- **GroupBox**: A container with a border and optional title.
- **FlowLayoutPanel**: A container that arranges controls in a flow, either horizontally or vertically.
- **TableLayoutPanel**: A container that arranges controls in rows and columns, providing a grid-like layout.

Container controls are particularly useful for creating organized and visually appealing UIs.

Custom Controls

While WinForms provides a variety of built-in controls, you can also create custom controls by deriving from existing ones or by creating entirely new controls. Custom controls allow you to encapsulate complex functionality and reuse it across your application or in different projects.

Working with Components

Components are reusable and self-contained pieces of functionality that you can add to your forms. Unlike controls, components are typically not visible to users but provide various services to your application. Examples of components in WinForms include:

- **Timer**: Allows you to execute code at specified intervals.
- **ToolTip**: Provides tooltips for controls to display additional information.
- **ErrorProvider**: Helps with error validation and error display for input controls.
- **ContextMenuStrip**: Creates context menus that appear when a user right-clicks a control.
- **PrintDocument**: Enables printing of documents or reports.

Components can be added to a form by dragging them from the Toolbox, and their properties can be configured through the Properties window.

Conclusion

Controls and components are the essential building blocks for creating functional and interactive user interfaces in WinForms applications. By understanding the available controls, configuring their properties, and utilizing container controls for layout, you can design effective and user-friendly interfaces. Additionally, components provide valuable services that enhance your application's functionality. In the next sections, we will delve into more advanced topics related to WinForms development, including data binding and working with data grids.

Section 5.5: Building a Complete GUI Application

In this section, we'll discuss the process of building a complete GUI application using Windows Forms (WinForms). We'll cover the essential steps and considerations to create a fully functional and user-friendly WinForms application.

Define Application Requirements

Before you start building your WinForms application, it's crucial to define clear requirements. Understand what the application is supposed to do, who the target users are, and what features and functionality are required. Create a list of user stories or use cases to guide your development process.

Create the User Interface

Design the user interface (UI) of your application using the WinForms visual designer in Visual Studio. This involves placing controls on forms, configuring their properties, and organizing them for a logical and intuitive user experience. Ensure that the UI adheres to usability and design principles for a polished look and feel.

Implement Functionality

Once the UI is designed, implement the functionality of your application. Write the code to respond to user interactions, handle events, and perform tasks based on the defined requirements. This may involve creating custom methods and classes to encapsulate specific functionality.

Data Management

If your application involves data management, consider how you will handle data storage and retrieval. You may need to connect to databases, read and write data files, or work with web services. WinForms provides tools and components for data binding, making it easier to connect UI elements to data sources.

Validation and Error Handling

Implement data validation and error handling to ensure data integrity and provide a robust user experience. Use validation controls, error providers, and custom validation logic to prevent incorrect data entry and provide meaningful error messages to users.

Testing

Thoroughly test your application to identify and resolve bugs and issues. Perform functional testing to verify that the application behaves as expected, and conduct usability testing to ensure the UI is intuitive and user-friendly. Debugging tools in Visual Studio can help identify and fix problems in your code.

Localization

If your application is intended for a global audience, consider localization and internationalization. Provide translations for different languages and cultures to make your application accessible to a broader user base. WinForms supports resource files for managing localized content.

Documentation and Help

Create documentation for your application, including user guides, manuals, and online help. Clear and concise documentation can assist users in understanding how to use your application effectively. You can also integrate context-sensitive help within the application using tooltips or context menus.

Deployment

Prepare your application for deployment to end-users. Create an installer or package the application for distribution. Consider the deployment platform, whether it's a standalone desktop application or a networked client-server application.

User Feedback

Collect user feedback and consider user suggestions for future updates and improvements to your application. Feedback can provide valuable insights into user needs and pain points, helping you refine and enhance your software over time.

Maintenance and Updates

After the initial release, plan for ongoing maintenance and updates to address issues, add new features, and ensure compatibility with evolving operating systems and dependencies. Regularly review and refactor your codebase to maintain code quality.

Building a complete GUI application with WinForms is a rewarding process that involves careful planning, design, and development. By following these steps and continuously iterating based on user feedback and changing requirements, you can create a successful and user-centric WinForms application.

Chapter 6: Cross-Platform Development with .NET Core

Section 6.1: Understanding .NET Core and .NET 5+

In this section, we'll explore the world of cross-platform development using .NET Core and the subsequent versions like .NET 5 and beyond. .NET Core is a powerful framework that allows developers to build applications that can run on various platforms, including Windows, macOS, and Linux. It is designed for modern, cloud-native applications and provides several key features:

1. Cross-Platform Compatibility

.NET Core is designed from the ground up to be cross-platform. This means you can write C# code and run it on Windows, macOS, or Linux without major modifications. This flexibility is essential for reaching a broad audience and deploying applications in different environments.

2. Improved Performance

.NET Core offers better performance compared to its predecessor, the .NET Framework. It includes the CoreCLR, a modern runtime that optimizes performance, making it suitable for high-performance applications. You can leverage the speed and efficiency of .NET Core for various types of projects.

3. Support for Containerization

Containerization is a popular technique for packaging applications and their dependencies into isolated containers. .NET Core supports containerization technologies like Docker, making it easy to create and deploy containerized applications. This is particularly useful in microservices and cloud-native architectures.

4. Side-by-Side Installation

Unlike the .NET Framework, which could lead to version conflicts, .NET Core allows side-by-side installations of different versions. This means you can develop and run applications that target specific .NET Core versions without worrying about affecting other applications on the same system.

5. Open-Source and Community-Driven

.NET Core is open-source and actively maintained by Microsoft. It also benefits from a vibrant community that contributes to its development. This openness allows developers to participate in shaping the framework's future and contributes to its rapid evolution.

6. Migration Paths

If you have existing .NET Framework applications, .NET Core provides migration paths to move them to the new platform. .NET 5 and later versions offer increased compatibility with existing libraries and APIs, easing the transition process.

7. Unified Platform

Starting with .NET 5, Microsoft aimed to unify the .NET ecosystem, bringing together .NET Core, .NET Framework, and Xamarin into a single platform called .NET 5. This unified platform simplifies development and reduces fragmentation.

To get started with .NET Core, you'll need to install the SDK and use tools like Visual Studio Code or Visual Studio for development. .NET Core supports various application types, including console applications, web applications, and cloud-native microservices.

In the following sections of this chapter, we'll delve deeper into specific aspects of cross-platform development with .NET Core, including building console applications, desktop applications, web development with ASP.NET Core, and mobile app development with Xamarin. Whether you're targeting cloud-based services or creating applications for multiple platforms, .NET Core provides a robust foundation for your projects.

Section 6.2: Building Cross-Platform Console Apps

In this section, we'll focus on building cross-platform console applications using .NET Core. Console applications are lightweight, text-based programs that run in a command-line interface (CLI). They are useful for a wide range of tasks, including automation, data processing, and system administration.

Creating a New Console Application

To create a new console application using .NET Core, follow these steps:

1. **Install the .NET SDK**: Ensure you have the .NET SDK installed on your system. You can download it from the official .NET website.
2. **Create a New Project**: Open your terminal or command prompt and navigate to the directory where you want to create the project. Use the following command to create a

new console application:

```
dotnet new console -n MyConsoleApp
```

This command creates a new console application named "MyConsoleApp."

1. **Open the Project**: Use a code editor of your choice, such as Visual Studio Code or Visual Studio, to open the project folder. You'll find a file named Program.cs, which contains the entry point for your application.
2. **Edit the Code**: In the Program.cs file, you'll see a Main method. This method is the starting point for your console application. You can write your application logic inside this method.

Writing Your First Console App

Let's write a simple "Hello, World!" program to get started. Replace the contents of the Main method with the following code:

```
using System;

namespace MyConsoleApp

{

class Program

{

static void Main(string[] args)

{

Console.WriteLine("Hello, World!");
```

```
}
}
}
```

This code imports the System namespace and uses the Console.WriteLine method to print "Hello, World!" to the console.

Building and Running the App

To build and run your console application, follow these steps:

1. In the terminal, navigate to your project's root directory.
2. Use the following command to build the application:

```
dotnet build
```

1. Once the build is successful, run the application using:

```
dotnet run
```

You should see the output "Hello, World!" displayed in the console.

Cross-Platform Execution

The beauty of .NET Core is its cross-platform compatibility. You can develop and run the same console application on Windows, macOS, and Linux without modification. This makes it easy to create tools and utilities that work seamlessly across different operating systems.

Handling Command-Line Arguments

Console applications often accept command-line arguments. You can access command-line arguments through the args parameter of the Main method. For example, if you run your application with the command:

```
dotnet run arg1 arg2
```

You can access the arguments in your code like this:

```
static void Main(string[] args)
{
foreach (var arg in args)
{
Console.WriteLine($"Argument: {arg}");
}
}
```

This code will print:

```
Argument: arg1
Argument: arg2
```

In summary, building cross-platform console applications with .NET Core is straightforward. You can leverage the power of C# and the versatility of the command line to create efficient and portable tools for various tasks. Whether you're automating system administration tasks or processing data, console applications are a valuable addition to your development toolkit.

Section 6.3: Creating Cross-Platform Desktop Applications

In this section, we'll explore how to create cross-platform desktop applications using .NET Core. While .NET Core was initially designed for server and console applications, it has evolved to support desktop applications as well. One of the technologies that enable this capability is the .NET Core Windows Presentation Foundation (WPF) framework.

What is .NET Core WPF?

.NET Core WPF is a cross-platform version of Windows Presentation Foundation, a popular technology for building Windows desktop applications. With .NET Core WPF, you can create native, feature-rich desktop applications that run on Windows, macOS, and Linux.

Prerequisites

Before you start building .NET Core WPF applications, make sure you have the following prerequisites:

1. **Install .NET Core SDK**: Ensure that you have the .NET Core SDK installed on your development machine. You can download it from the official .NET website.
2. **Choose an IDE**: You can use Visual Studio, Visual Studio Code, or any other code editor of your choice. Visual Studio provides a rich development experience for WPF applications.
3. **Create a New WPF Project**: To create a new .NET Core WPF project, use the following command:

```
dotnet new wpf -n MyWpfApp
```

This command creates a new WPF project named "MyWpfApp."

Building a Simple WPF Application

Let's create a basic .NET Core WPF application to get started. Open the project in your chosen IDE and navigate to the MainWindow.xaml file. This file defines the user interface of your application.

Here's a simple XAML code snippet for a window with a button:

```
<Window x:Class="MyWpfApp.MainWindow"

xmlns="http://schemas.microsoft.com/winfx/2006/xaml/presentation"

xmlns:x="http://schemas.microsoft.com/winfx/2006/xaml"

Title="Hello WPF" Height="350" Width="525">

<Grid>

<Button Content="Click Me" HorizontalAlignment="Center" VerticalAlignment="Center" Click="Button_Click"/>

</Grid>

</Window>
```

This XAML code defines a window with a button labeled "Click Me."

Next, navigate to the MainWindow.xaml.cs file to add the code-behind logic. In the code-behind file, add the event handler for the button click event:

```
using System.Windows;

namespace MyWpfApp

{

public partial class MainWindow : Window

{

public MainWindow()

{

InitializeComponent();

}

private void Button_Click(object sender, RoutedEventArgs e)

{

MessageBox.Show("Hello, WPF!");

}

}

}
```

This code attaches an event handler to the button's click event, which displays a message box with the text "Hello, WPF!" when the button is clicked.

Running the WPF Application

To run your .NET Core WPF application, follow these steps:

1. Build the application using the following command:

```
dotnet build
```

1. Run the application:

```
dotnet run
```

You should see a window with the "Click Me" button. When you click the button, a message box displaying "Hello, WPF!" will appear.

Cross-Platform Execution

The remarkable aspect of .NET Core WPF is its ability to run on multiple platforms. You can develop and test your application on one platform and then deploy it to Windows, macOS, and Linux without modification. This makes it easier to reach a broader audience with your desktop applications.

In summary, .NET Core WPF enables you to create cross-platform desktop applications with a familiar development experience. Whether you're building utilities, productivity tools, or more complex desktop software, .NET Core WPF empowers you to target a wide range of operating systems and deliver high-quality desktop applications.

Section 6.4: Web Development with ASP.NET Core

In this section, we'll explore web development using ASP.NET Core, another versatile framework within the .NET ecosystem. ASP.NET Core allows you to build modern, high-performance web applications that can run on various platforms, making it a powerful choice for cross-platform web development.

Key Features of ASP.NET Core

ASP.NET Core offers several key features that make it a compelling choice for web development:

1. **Cross-Platform Compatibility**: ASP.NET Core applications can run on Windows, macOS, and Linux, making it suitable for diverse server environments.
2. **High Performance**: ASP.NET Core is designed for high performance, with optimizations that reduce latency and improve throughput. This is crucial for building responsive web applications.
3. **Modular and Lightweight**: ASP.NET Core is modular, allowing you to include only the components your application needs. This results in smaller, more efficient applications.
4. **Open Source**: ASP.NET Core is open source and actively maintained by Microsoft and the community. This openness fosters innovation and ensures ongoing support.
5. **Integrated Dependency Injection**: ASP.NET Core includes built-in dependency injection, making it easy to manage and inject dependencies into your application components.
6. **Razor Pages and MVC**: ASP.NET Core supports both Razor Pages and Model-View-Controller (MVC) for building web applications. You can choose the approach that best suits your project's requirements.

Getting Started with ASP.NET Core

To get started with ASP.NET Core development, follow these steps:

1. **Install the .NET SDK**: Ensure you have the .NET SDK installed on your system. You can download it from the

official .NET website.

2. **Create a New ASP.NET Core Project**: Use the following command to create a new ASP.NET Core project:

```
dotnet new web -n MyWebApp
```

This command creates a new web application named "MyWebApp."

1. **Open the Project**: Use your preferred code editor to open the project folder. You'll find a startup file named Startup.cs and other project files.
2. **Build and Run the Application**: Build the application using dotnet build and run it with dotnet run. By default, the application runs on http://localhost:5000.

Creating a Simple Web Page

To create a simple web page in ASP.NET Core, you can use Razor Pages, which provide a straightforward way to combine HTML and C# code. Here's an example of a Razor Page that displays "Hello, ASP.NET Core!" on the homepage:

```
@page

<!DOCTYPE html>

<html>

<head>

<title>My ASP.NET Core Page</title>

</head>

<body>
```

```
<h1>Hello, ASP.NET Core!</h1>

</body>

</html>
```

This Razor Page defines a basic HTML structure and uses @page to indicate that it's a Razor Page. The @page directive associates the page with a URL route, making it accessible as the homepage.

Adding Routes and Controllers

For more complex web applications, you can define routes and controllers to handle different requests. Routes map URLs to controller actions, allowing you to execute specific code when a user visits a particular URL. Here's an example of defining a route and a controller action in ASP.NET Core:

```
using Microsoft.AspNetCore.Mvc;

namespace MyWebApp.Controllers

{

public class HomeController : Controller

{

public IActionResult Index()

{

return View();

}

}
```

```
}
```

In this example, the HomeController contains an Index action that returns a view. Views are typically Razor Pages or templates that render the HTML content to be sent to the client.

Running the ASP.NET Core Web Application

To run your ASP.NET Core web application, follow these steps:

1. Build the application using dotnet build.
2. Run the application with dotnet run. By default, it starts the web server, and your application is accessible at http://localhost:5000.
3. Open a web browser and navigate to http://localhost:5000 to see your application in action.

Cross-Platform Web Development

ASP.NET Core's cross-platform compatibility means you can develop web applications on your preferred platform and deploy them to various server environments, including Windows, macOS, and Linux. This flexibility makes it an excellent choice for building web applications that reach a broad audience.

In summary, ASP.NET Core empowers developers to build modern, high-performance web applications with cross-platform capabilities. Whether you're creating simple web pages or complex web applications with controllers and routes, ASP.NET Core provides the tools and flexibility needed to deliver exceptional web experiences.

Section 6.5: Mobile App Development with Xamarin

Xamarin is a powerful framework for building cross-platform mobile applications using C# and .NET. It allows you to write your app's business logic once and deploy it to both iOS and Android platforms, saving time and effort compared to developing separate native apps. In this section, we'll explore mobile app development with Xamarin.

Key Features of Xamarin

Xamarin provides several key features that make it a popular choice for cross-platform mobile development:

1. **Single Codebase**: With Xamarin, you write your app's code in C#, and a large portion of it can be shared between iOS and Android. This means you maintain a single codebase for both platforms.
2. **Native Performance**: Xamarin allows you to access native APIs and components, ensuring your app's performance is on par with native applications.
3. **XAML for UI**: Xamarin uses XAML for defining the user interface, making it easier to design cross-platform UIs with a familiar markup language.
4. **Integration with Visual Studio**: Xamarin integrates seamlessly with Visual Studio, Microsoft's popular IDE, making it easy to develop, debug, and test mobile apps.
5. **Large Ecosystem**: Xamarin benefits from the .NET ecosystem, with access to libraries and packages that enhance your app's functionality.

Getting Started with Xamarin

To begin mobile app development with Xamarin, follow these steps:

1. **Install Visual Studio**: If you haven't already, install Visual Studio, including the Xamarin workload.
2. **Create a New Xamarin Project**: Open Visual Studio and create a new Xamarin.Forms project. Xamarin.Forms is a UI framework that allows you to define your app's user interface once and deploy it to multiple platforms.
3. **Design the User Interface**: Use XAML to design the user interface of your app. Xamarin.Forms provides a wide range of controls and layouts to create cross-platform UIs.
4. **Write the App Logic**: Write your app's business logic in C#. You can use shared code for common functionality and platform-specific code when needed.
5. **Test and Debug**: Use the built-in debugging tools in Visual Studio to test your app on both iOS and Android emulators. Xamarin provides excellent support for debugging, making it easier to catch and fix issues.
6. **Publish to App Stores**: Once your app is ready, you can publish it to the Apple App Store and Google Play Store. Xamarin simplifies the deployment process.

Creating a Simple Xamarin.Forms App

Here's a basic example of a Xamarin.Forms app with a simple UI:

```
<?xml version="1.0" encoding="utf-8" ?>

<ContentPage xmlns="http://xamarin.com/schemas/2014/forms"

xmlns:x="http://schemas.microsoft.com/winfx/2009/xaml"

x:Class="MyApp.MainPage">
```

```
<StackLayout>
<Label Text="Welcome to Xamarin.Forms!"
VerticalOptions="CenterAndExpand"
HorizontalOptions="CenterAndExpand" />
<Button Text="Click Me"
Clicked="Button_Clicked" />
</StackLayout>
</ContentPage>
```

In this XAML code, we define a simple page with a label and a button. When the button is clicked, we'll display a message.

Next, in the code-behind file (MainPage.xaml.cs), you can add the event handler for the button click:

```
using System;
using Xamarin.Forms;
namespace MyApp
{
public partial class MainPage : ContentPage
{
public MainPage()
{
InitializeComponent();
```

```
}
private void Button_Clicked(object sender, EventArgs e)
{
DisplayAlert("Hello", "Welcome to Xamarin.Forms!", "OK");
}
}
}
```

In this C# code, we handle the button click event by displaying an alert with a welcome message.

Running Xamarin Apps on Emulators

To test your Xamarin app on emulators, follow these steps:

1. In Visual Studio, select the target platform (iOS or Android) and emulator device from the toolbar.
2. Click the "Start Debugging" button, and Visual Studio will launch the selected emulator with your app.
3. You can interact with the app on the emulator just like you would on a physical device.

Cross-Platform Mobile Development Made Easier

Xamarin simplifies cross-platform mobile app development by allowing you to leverage your C# skills and share code between iOS and Android. Whether you're building a simple utility app or a complex mobile application, Xamarin provides the tools and framework to streamline the development process and deliver high-quality apps to a broad audience.

Chapter 7: File Handling and Serialization

Section 7.1: Reading and Writing Files in C

File handling is a fundamental aspect of many software applications. In C#, you can perform various file operations, including reading from and writing to files. This section explores how to work with files in C#.

Reading Text Files

To read the contents of a text file in C#, you can use the File.ReadAllText method. Here's an example:

```
using System;

using System.IO;

class Program

{

static void Main()

{

string filePath = "sample.txt";

try

{

string fileContents = File.ReadAllText(filePath);

Console.WriteLine("File Contents:");
```

```
Console.WriteLine(fileContents);
}
catch (FileNotFoundException)
{
Console.WriteLine($"File not found: {filePath}");
}
catch (IOException e)
{
Console.WriteLine($"An error occurred: {e.Message}");
}
}
}
```

In this example, we use File.ReadAllText to read the contents of the "sample.txt" file and then display them on the console. We also handle exceptions, such as FileNotFoundException and IOException, that can occur during file operations.

Writing to Text Files

To write data to a text file, you can use the File.WriteAllText method. Here's an example:

```
using System;
using System.IO;
class Program
```

```
{
static void Main()
{
string filePath = "output.txt";
string content = "This is some sample text.";
try
{
File.WriteAllText(filePath, content);
Console.WriteLine("File written successfully!");
}
catch (IOException e)
{
Console.WriteLine($"An error occurred: {e.Message}");
}
}
}
```

In this example, we use File.WriteAllText to write the specified content to the "output.txt" file. Again, we handle potential IOExceptions that may occur during the file write operation.

Reading and Writing Binary Files

While the previous examples focused on text files, you can also read and write binary files in C# using FileStream. Binary files are used for a wide range of purposes, including storing images, audio, and other non-textual data.

Here's a simple example of reading and writing a binary file:

```
using System;

using System.IO;

class Program

{

static void Main()

{

string filePath = "binary.dat";

// Write binary data to a file

byte[] dataToWrite = { 0x48, 0x65, 0x6C, 0x6C, 0x6F }; // "Hello" in hexadecimal

using (FileStream fs = new FileStream(filePath, FileMode.Create))

{

fs.Write(dataToWrite, 0, dataToWrite.Length);

Console.WriteLine("Binary data written successfully!");

}

// Read binary data from a file
```

```
byte[] dataRead = new byte[dataToWrite.Length];
using (FileStream fs = new FileStream(filePath, FileMode.Open))
{
fs.Read(dataRead, 0, dataRead.Length);
Console.WriteLine("Read Binary Data:");
Console.WriteLine(BitConverter.ToString(dataRead)); // Output hexadecimal representation
}
}
}
```

In this example, we use a FileStream to write and read binary data to and from a file. We write the "Hello" string in hexadecimal format to the file and then read it back, displaying the hexadecimal representation.

Handling File Paths

When working with files, it's essential to handle file paths correctly, especially if your application needs to work on different platforms. You can use Path.Combine and other methods from the System.IO namespace to construct and manipulate file paths in a platform-independent way.

File handling is a fundamental skill in C# development, whether you're dealing with configuration files, log files, or any other type of data persistence. Understanding how to read and write files is essential for building robust and data-centric applications.

Section 7.2: Working with Streams and Readers/Writers

In C#, working with streams and readers/writers provides more flexibility and control when dealing with file I/O operations. Streams are a fundamental concept for reading and writing data, while readers and writers simplify text-based operations. This section delves into the usage of streams and readers/writers in C#.

Streams

A stream is a sequence of bytes that can be read from or written to. In C#, the Stream class and its derivatives, such as FileStream, MemoryStream, and NetworkStream, provide various ways to work with data streams. Streams are particularly useful when handling large files or when you need to manipulate data byte by byte.

Here's a simple example of reading data from a file using a FileStream:

```
using System;

using System.IO;

class Program

{

static void Main()

{

string filePath = "sample.txt";

try

{
```

```
using (FileStream fs = new FileStream(filePath, FileMode.Open))
{
byte[] buffer = new byte[1024];
int bytesRead;
while ((bytesRead = fs.Read(buffer, 0, buffer.Length)) > 0)
{
// Process the read data here
Console.Write(Encoding.UTF8.GetString(buffer, 0, bytesRead));
}
}
}
catch (FileNotFoundException)
{
Console.WriteLine($"File not found: {filePath}");
}
catch (IOException e)
{
Console.WriteLine($"An error occurred: {e.Message}");
}
}
```

```
}
```

In this example, we use a FileStream to open and read a file byte by byte. We read data into a buffer and process it as needed.

Readers and Writers

While streams are versatile, they can be low-level when dealing with text-based data. Readers and writers, such as StreamReader and StreamWriter, provide higher-level abstractions that make it easier to work with text data.

Here's how to read a text file using a StreamReader:

```
using System;

using System.IO;

class Program

{

static void Main()

{

string filePath = "sample.txt";

try

{

using (StreamReader reader = new StreamReader(filePath))

{

string line;

while ((line = reader.ReadLine()) != null)
```

```
{
Console.WriteLine(line);
}
}
}
catch (FileNotFoundException)
{
Console.WriteLine($"File not found: {filePath}");
}
catch (IOException e)
{
Console.WriteLine($"An error occurred: {e.Message}");
}
}
}
```

In this example, we use a StreamReader to read text from a file line by line. The ReadLine method simplifies reading text-based data.

Writing text data to a file is similarly straightforward with a StreamWriter:

```
using System;
using System.IO;
```

```
class Program
{
static void Main()
{
string filePath = "output.txt";
try
{
using (StreamWriter writer = new StreamWriter(filePath))
{
writer.WriteLine("This is line 1.");
writer.WriteLine("This is line 2.");
}
Console.WriteLine("Text written successfully!");
}
catch (IOException e)
{
Console.WriteLine($"An error occurred: {e.Message}");
}
}
}
```

Here, we use a StreamWriter to write text data to a file. The WriteLine method simplifies writing lines of text.

Choosing Between Streams and Readers/Writers

When working with files in C#, consider your specific use case. Streams are ideal for binary data or low-level manipulation, while readers and writers are better suited for text-based operations. The choice depends on the level of control and convenience your application requires for file I/O.

Section 7.3: Serialization and Deserialization

Serialization is the process of converting complex data structures, such as objects, into a format that can be easily stored, transmitted, or reconstructed. In C#, serialization is commonly used for tasks like saving objects to a file or sending them over a network. Deserialization is the reverse process, where serialized data is converted back into its original form. This section explores serialization and deserialization techniques in C#.

Binary Serialization

C# provides built-in support for binary serialization through the System.Runtime.Serialization.Formatters.Binary namespace. You can serialize objects and write them to a binary file, which can later be deserialized to recreate the original object.

Here's a basic example of binary serialization and deserialization:

```
using System;

using System.IO;

using System.Runtime.Serialization.Formatters.Binary;
```

```
[Serializable]
class Person
{
public string Name { get; set; }
public int Age { get; set; }
}
class Program
{
static void Main()
{
// Serialization
Person person = new Person { Name = "Alice", Age = 30 };
BinaryFormatter formatter = new BinaryFormatter();
using (FileStream fs = new FileStream("person.dat", FileMode.Create))
{
formatter.Serialize(fs, person);
Console.WriteLine("Object serialized and saved.");
}
// Deserialization
```

```
using (FileStream fs = new FileStream("person.dat", FileMode.Open))

{

Person deserializedPerson = (Person)formatter.Deserialize(fs);

Console.WriteLine($"Name: {deserializedPerson.Name}, Age: {deserializedPerson.Age}");

}

}

}
```

In this example, we define a Person class and mark it as [Serializable]. We then serialize an instance of this class to a binary file using BinaryFormatter, and later, we deserialize it to retrieve the original object.

XML and JSON Serialization

Apart from binary serialization, C# also supports XML and JSON serialization, which are often used for data exchange between applications or platforms. You can use XmlSerializer and JsonSerializer from the System.Xml.Serialization and System.Text.Json namespaces, respectively.

Here's an example of XML serialization and deserialization:

```
using System;

using System.IO;

using System.Xml.Serialization;
```

```
[Serializable]

public class Person

{

public string Name { get; set; }

public int Age { get; set; }

}

class Program

{

static void Main()

{

// Serialization to XML

Person person = new Person { Name = "Bob", Age = 25 };

XmlSerializer xmlSerializer = new XmlSerializer(typeof(Person));

using (FileStream fs = new FileStream("person.xml", FileMode.Create))

{

xmlSerializer.Serialize(fs, person);

Console.WriteLine("Object serialized as XML.");

}

// Deserialization from XML
```

```
using (FileStream fs = new FileStream("person.xml", FileMode.Open))

{

Person deserializedPerson = (Person)xmlSerializer.Deserialize(fs);

Console.WriteLine($"Name: {deserializedPerson.Name}, Age: {deserializedPerson.Age}");

}

}

}
```

In this XML serialization example, we use XmlSerializer to serialize and deserialize a Person object to and from an XML file.

JSON serialization and deserialization can be achieved similarly using JsonSerializer from the System.Text.Json namespace. These serialization formats are more human-readable and widely used in web APIs and data interchange.

Serialization and deserialization are essential techniques in C# for saving and retrieving application data and sharing data between different components and systems. Choosing the appropriate serialization format depends on your specific use case and requirements.

Section 7.4: Handling XML and JSON Data

XML (Extensible Markup Language) and JSON (JavaScript Object Notation) are two widely used data interchange formats. In C#, you can work with both XML and JSON data for various purposes, such as configuration files, web service communication, and data storage. This section explores how to handle XML and JSON data in C#.

Working with XML Data

C# provides libraries for parsing and manipulating XML data. The System.Xml namespace includes classes like XmlDocument, XmlReader, and XmlWriter for working with XML data.

Here's an example of reading and writing XML data using XmlDocument:

```
using System;

using System.Xml;

class Program

{

static void Main()

{

// Creating an XML document

XmlDocument xmlDoc = new XmlDocument();

xmlDoc.LoadXml("<book><title>C# Programming</title><author>John Doe</author></book>");

// Reading XML data

XmlNode titleNode = xmlDoc.SelectSingleNode("/book/title");

string title = titleNode.InnerText;
```

```
XmlNode authorNode = xmlDoc.SelectSingleNode("/book/author");

string author = authorNode.InnerText;

Console.WriteLine($"Title: {title}");

Console.WriteLine($"Author: {author}");

// Modifying XML data

titleNode.InnerText = "Advanced C# Programming";

// Saving the modified XML

xmlDoc.Save("book.xml");

Console.WriteLine("XML data saved.");

}

}
```

In this example, we create an XML document, read data from it, modify the data, and then save it back to a file.

Working with JSON Data

To work with JSON data in C#, you can use the System.Text.Json namespace. It provides classes like JsonSerializer for serialization and deserialization of JSON data.

Here's an example of working with JSON data:

```
using System;

using System.Text.Json;

class Program
```

```
{
public class Person
{
public string Name { get; set; }
public int Age { get; set; }
}
static void Main()
{
// Serialization to JSON
Person person = new Person { Name = "Alice", Age = 28 };
string json = JsonSerializer.Serialize(person);
Console.WriteLine($"JSON: {json}");
// Deserialization from JSON
Person deserializedPerson = JsonSerializer.Deserialize<Person>(json);
Console.WriteLine($"Name: {deserializedPerson.Name}, Age: {deserializedPerson.Age}");
}
}
```

In this JSON example, we define a Person class, serialize an instance of it to JSON, and then deserialize it back to a C# object.

Both XML and JSON are versatile formats for data exchange. Choose the one that best suits your application's requirements and integrates seamlessly with other systems or services you may be interacting with. C# provides excellent support for both formats, making it easy to work with XML and JSON data.

Section 7.5: Database Connectivity and ADO.NET

Database connectivity is a crucial aspect of many software applications. C# provides the ADO.NET (ActiveX Data Objects for .NET) framework for interacting with relational databases. ADO.NET allows you to connect to databases, execute queries, and retrieve and manipulate data. In this section, we will explore how to work with databases using ADO.NET in C#.

Connecting to a Database

To connect to a database using ADO.NET, you need to specify a connection string that contains information about the database server, authentication credentials, and the database itself. Here's an example of connecting to a SQL Server database:

```
using System;

using System.Data.SqlClient;

class Program

{

static void Main()

{
```

```
string connectionString = "Server=myServer;Database=myDatabase;User Id=myUser;Password=myPassword;";

using (SqlConnection connection = new SqlConnection(connectionString))

{

connection.Open();

Console.WriteLine("Connected to the database.");

// Perform database operations here

connection.Close();

Console.WriteLine("Connection closed.");

}

}

}
```

In this example, we create a SqlConnection object and open the connection using the specified connection string. You should replace myServer, myDatabase, myUser, and myPassword with the actual database server information and credentials.

Executing SQL Queries

ADO.NET allows you to execute SQL queries against the database. You can use SqlCommand to define and execute SQL commands. Here's an example of executing a simple SQL query to retrieve data from a SQL Server database:

```
using System;

using System.Data.SqlClient;

class Program

{

static void Main()

{

string connectionString = "Server=myServer;Database=myDatabase;User Id=myUser;Password=myPassword;";

using (SqlConnection connection = new SqlConnection(connectionString))

{

connection.Open();

Console.WriteLine("Connected to the database.");

// Execute a SQL query

string query = "SELECT FirstName, LastName FROM Employees";

using (SqlCommand command = new SqlCommand(query, connection))

{

SqlDataReader reader = command.ExecuteReader();

while (reader.Read())

{
```

```
Console.WriteLine($"First Name: {reader["FirstName"]}, Last Name: {reader["LastName"]}");

}

reader.Close();

}

connection.Close();

Console.WriteLine("Connection closed.");

}

}

}
```

In this example, we execute a SELECT query to retrieve employee data from a table called Employees and display the results.

Parameterized Queries and Security

When working with SQL queries, it's essential to use parameterized queries to prevent SQL injection attacks. Parameterized queries separate SQL code from user input, making it more secure. Here's an example of a parameterized query:

```
using System;

using System.Data.SqlClient;

class Program

{

static void Main()
```

```
{
string connectionString = "Server=myServer;Database=myDatabase;User Id=myUser;Password=myPassword;";
using (SqlConnection connection = new SqlConnection(connectionString))
{
connection.Open();
Console.WriteLine("Connected to the database.");
// Parameterized query
string query = "SELECT FirstName, LastName FROM Employees WHERE Department = @Department";
using (SqlCommand command = new SqlCommand(query, connection))
{
command.Parameters.AddWithValue("@Department", "HR");
SqlDataReader reader = command.ExecuteReader();
while (reader.Read())
{
Console.WriteLine($"First Name: {reader["FirstName"]}, Last Name: {reader["LastName"]}");
}
```

```
reader.Close();

}

connection.Close();

Console.WriteLine("Connection closed.");

}

}

}
```

In this example, we use the @Department parameter to filter the results based on the department specified in the parameter.

ADO.NET is a versatile framework for database connectivity in C#. It supports various database systems, including SQL Server, MySQL, Oracle, and more. Understanding ADO.NET is crucial for building applications that interact with databases and manage data effectively.

Chapter 8: Networking and Web Services

Section 8.1: Introduction to Networking in C

Networking plays a vital role in modern software development, enabling applications to communicate over the internet, local networks, and various protocols. C# provides extensive support for network programming through libraries and classes in the .NET Framework. In this section, we will introduce you to networking in C# and explore how to perform basic network operations.

Understanding Network Communication

Network communication involves the exchange of data between different devices or applications. This communication can be between a client and a server, two peers in a peer-to-peer network, or even communication with external web services. In C#, you can use classes from the System.Net namespace to work with network-related tasks.

Here are some common scenarios in which network communication is essential:

1. **Client-Server Communication:** Applications often follow a client-server architecture, where the client requests information or services from a server. This is common in web applications, where a web browser (client) communicates with a web server to fetch web pages or data.
2. **Peer-to-Peer Communication:** In peer-to-peer networks, devices communicate directly with each other without a

centralized server. This is seen in applications like file sharing or online gaming.

3. **Web Service Integration:** Many modern applications integrate with web services to access data or functionality provided by external services. This includes using APIs (Application Programming Interfaces) to interact with services such as social media platforms, payment gateways, and more.

Basic Networking Tasks

C# provides classes like TcpClient, TcpListener, UdpClient, and HttpWebRequest to handle various aspects of network communication. Here's a brief overview of some basic networking tasks you can perform in C#:

- **TCP and UDP Communication:** You can use TcpClient and TcpListener for TCP (Transmission Control Protocol) communication and UdpClient for UDP (User Datagram Protocol) communication. These classes allow you to establish connections, send and receive data, and handle network streams.

- **HTTP Communication:** The HttpWebRequest and HttpWebResponse classes provide high-level abstractions for sending HTTP requests and receiving responses. This is useful for interacting with RESTful APIs and web services.

- **Socket Programming:** For more advanced network tasks, C# allows low-level socket programming using the Socket class. This is especially useful when you need fine-grained control over network operations.

- **Asynchronous Programming:** Networking operations often involve waiting for responses, which can lead to blocking code. C# supports asynchronous programming using the async and await keywords, allowing you to perform network operations without blocking the main thread.

- **Error Handling:** Proper error handling is crucial in network programming. You need to handle exceptions that may occur during network operations gracefully.

In the upcoming sections of this chapter, we will delve deeper into these topics and provide practical examples of network programming in C#. Understanding network communication is essential for building applications that interact with remote services or devices, making it a valuable skill for C# developers.

Section 8.2: Creating TCP and UDP Clients and Servers

In this section, we will explore how to create both TCP (Transmission Control Protocol) and UDP (User Datagram Protocol) clients and servers using C#. TCP and UDP are two of the most commonly used transport layer protocols for network communication, each with its own characteristics and use cases.

TCP Communication

TCP is a connection-oriented protocol that provides reliable, stream-oriented communication. It ensures that data sent from one end is received by the other end in the correct order and without loss. TCP is commonly used for applications where data integrity is crucial, such as web browsing, email, and file transfer.

Creating a TCP Server

To create a TCP server in C#, you can use the TcpListener class. Here's a simple example of how to create a TCP server that listens for incoming connections and handles client requests:

```
using System;

using System.Net;

using System.Net.Sockets;

using System.Text;

class TcpServer

{

static void Main()

{

// Set the IP address and port to listen on

IPAddress ipAddress = IPAddress.Parse("127.0.0.1");

int port = 12345;

// Create a TcpListener

TcpListener server = new TcpListener(ipAddress, port);

// Start listening for incoming connections

server.Start();

Console.WriteLine("TCP Server is listening...");

while (true)
```

```
{
// Accept the client connection
TcpClient client = server.AcceptTcpClient();
Console.WriteLine("Client connected");
// Get the client's network stream for reading and writing
NetworkStream stream = client.GetStream();
// Read data from the client
byte[] buffer = new byte[1024];
int bytesRead = stream.Read(buffer, 0, buffer.Length);
string dataReceived = Encoding.ASCII.GetString(buffer, 0,
bytesRead);
Console.WriteLine($"Received: {dataReceived}");
// Send a response to the client
string responseMessage = "Hello from the server!";
byte[] responseData =
Encoding.ASCII.GetBytes(responseMessage);
stream.Write(responseData, 0, responseData.Length);
// Close the client connection
client.Close();
Console.WriteLine("Client disconnected");
}
```

```
}
}
```

In this example, the server listens on IP address 127.0.0.1 and port 12345. It accepts incoming client connections, reads data from the client, sends a response, and then closes the connection.

Creating a TCP Client

To create a TCP client in C#, you can use the TcpClient class. Here's a simple example of how to create a TCP client that connects to a server and sends data:

```
using System;
using System.Net.Sockets;
using System.Text;
class TcpClientExample
{
static void Main()
{
// Set the server's IP address and port
string serverIp = "127.0.0.1";
int serverPort = 12345;
using (TcpClient client = new TcpClient(serverIp, serverPort))
{
```

```
Console.WriteLine("Connected to the server");
// Get the network stream for reading and writing
NetworkStream stream = client.GetStream();
// Send data to the server
string message = "Hello from the client!";
byte[] data = Encoding.ASCII.GetBytes(message);
stream.Write(data, 0, data.Length);
// Read the server's response
byte[] buffer = new byte[1024];
int bytesRead = stream.Read(buffer, 0, buffer.Length);
string response = Encoding.ASCII.GetString(buffer, 0, bytesRead);
Console.WriteLine($"Server Response: {response}");
}
}
}
```

In this example, the client connects to the server using the specified IP address and port, sends a message, and receives a response.

UDP Communication

UDP is a connectionless protocol that provides fast, lightweight communication. Unlike TCP, UDP does not guarantee data delivery or order. It is often used in scenarios where low overhead and real-time communication are more important than reliability, such as online gaming and streaming.

Creating a UDP Server and Client

To create a UDP server and client in C#, you can use the UdpClient class. Here's a simple example of a UDP server that listens for incoming datagrams and a UDP client that sends datagrams to the server:

```
using System;

using System.Net;

using System.Net.Sockets;

using System.Text;

class UdpServerAndClient

{

static void Main()

{

int port = 12345;

// UDP server

using (UdpClient server = new UdpClient(port))

{

Console.WriteLine("UDP Server is listening...");

IPEndPoint clientEndPoint = new IPEndPoint(IPAddress.Any, 0);
```

```
while (true)
{
byte[] receivedData = server.Receive(ref clientEndPoint);
string message = Encoding.ASCII.GetString(receivedData);
Console.WriteLine($"Received from {clientEndPoint}: {message}");
// Respond to the client
string responseMessage = "Hello from the UDP server!";
byte[] responseData = Encoding.ASCII.GetBytes(responseMessage);
server.Send(responseData, responseData.Length, clientEndPoint);
}
}
// UDP client
using (UdpClient client = new UdpClient())
{
string serverIp = "127.0.0.1";
IPEndPoint serverEndPoint = new IPEndPoint(IPAddress.Parse(serverIp), port);
// Send a message to the server
string message = "Hello from the UDP client!";
byte[] data = Encoding.ASCII.GetBytes(message);
```

```
client.Send(data, data.Length, serverEndPoint);

// Receive a response from the server

byte[] receivedData = client.Receive(ref serverEndPoint);

string response = Encoding.ASCII.GetString(receivedData);

Console.WriteLine($"Received from server: {response}");

}

}

}
```

In this example, we create a UDP server that listens on port 12345 and a UDP client that sends a message to the server's IP address and port. The server receives the message, responds to the client, and displays the received data.

Understanding TCP and UDP communication is essential for building networked applications and services. Depending on your application's requirements, you can choose the appropriate protocol to ensure the desired level of reliability and performance.

Section 8.3: Building RESTful Web Services

In this section, we will delve into the world of building RESTful web services using C#. REST (Representational State Transfer) is an architectural style for designing networked applications. RESTful web services use HTTP requests to perform CRUD (Create, Read, Update, Delete) operations on resources and are widely used for building APIs (Application Programming Interfaces) that enable communication between different systems.

Principles of RESTful Design

Before we start building RESTful web services, it's essential to understand the key principles of RESTful design:

1. **Resource-Based:** In REST, everything is treated as a resource, and each resource is identified by a unique URI (Uniform Resource Identifier). Resources can represent objects, data, or services.
2. **HTTP Methods:** RESTful services use HTTP methods to perform operations on resources. The most common HTTP methods used in REST are GET (retrieve), POST (create), PUT (update), and DELETE (delete).
3. **Stateless:** Each request to a RESTful service should contain all the information needed to understand and process the request. The server should not rely on the client's state. This enables scalability and reliability.
4. **Representation:** Resources can have multiple representations, such as JSON, XML, or HTML. Clients request a specific representation using content negotiation (typically via HTTP headers).
5. **Uniform Interface:** RESTful services have a uniform and predictable interface, making it easier for clients to interact with them.

Building a Simple RESTful Service

Let's create a simple RESTful service that manages a list of books. We will implement CRUD operations (Create, Read, Update, Delete) for the books resource.

Creating a RESTful Web API Project

1. Open Visual Studio and create a new project.
2. Select the "ASP.NET Core Web Application" template.
3. Choose the "API" template, which will set up a basic RESTful API project.

Implementing CRUD Operations

In the generated project, you will find a Controllers folder containing a ValuesController.cs file. Let's modify it to manage books.

Here's a simplified example of the controller:

```
using System.Collections.Generic;

using Microsoft.AspNetCore.Mvc;

[Route("api/books")]

[ApiController]

public class BooksController : ControllerBase

{

private List<Book> _books = new List<Book>

{

new Book { Id = 1, Title = "Book 1" },

new Book { Id = 2, Title = "Book 2" },

new Book { Id = 3, Title = "Book 3" }
```

```
};
[HttpGet]
public ActionResult<IEnumerable<Book>> Get()
{
return Ok(_books);
}
[HttpGet("{id}")]
public ActionResult<Book> Get(int id)
{
var book = _books.FirstOrDefault(b => b.Id == id);
if (book == null)
return NotFound();
return Ok(book);
}
[HttpPost]
public ActionResult<Book> Post([FromBody] Book book)
{
book.Id = _books.Count + 1;
_books.Add(book);
return CreatedAtAction(nameof(Get), new { id = book.Id }, book);
```

```
}
[HttpPut("{id}")]
public IActionResult Put(int id, [FromBody] Book book)
{
var existingBook = _books.FirstOrDefault(b => b.Id == id);
if (existingBook == null)
return NotFound();
existingBook.Title = book.Title;
return NoContent();
}
[HttpDelete("{id}")]
public IActionResult Delete(int id)
{
var bookToRemove = _books.FirstOrDefault(b => b.Id == id);
if (bookToRemove == null)
return NotFound();
_books.Remove(bookToRemove);
return NoContent();
}
}
```

```
public class Book
{
public int Id { get; set; }
public string Title { get; set; }
}
```

In this example, we define a BooksController that handles HTTP GET, POST, PUT, and DELETE requests for the /api/books endpoint. The controller manages a list of books in-memory for simplicity.

Testing the RESTful Service

You can test the RESTful service using tools like Postman or by sending HTTP requests from your application. Here are some sample requests:

- GET /api/books: Retrieve all books.
- GET /api/books/1: Retrieve book with ID 1.
- POST /api/books: Create a new book.
- PUT /api/books/2: Update book with ID 2.
- DELETE /api/books/3: Delete book with ID 3.

Building RESTful web services in C# enables you to create APIs that can be consumed by various clients, including web applications, mobile apps, and other services. Understanding RESTful design principles is essential for designing scalable and maintainable APIs.

Section 8.4: Consuming Web APIs

In this section, we will explore how to consume web APIs in C#. Consuming external web APIs is a common task in software development, allowing your application to fetch data or interact with services provided by other applications over the internet. We'll discuss various methods and libraries available for making HTTP requests and processing API responses in C#.

Using HttpClient for Making HTTP Requests

The System.Net.Http.HttpClient class is a powerful library for making HTTP requests in C#. It provides the necessary tools to send GET, POST, PUT, and DELETE requests and handle responses from web APIs. Below is a basic example of how to use HttpClient to make a GET request and process the response:

```
using System;

using System.Net.Http;

using System.Threading.Tasks;

class Program

{

static async Task Main()

{

using (HttpClient client = new HttpClient())

{

try
```

```
{
HttpResponseMessage response = await client.GetAsync("https://api.example.com/data");
response.EnsureSuccessStatusCode(); // Ensure a successful response
string responseBody = await response.Content.ReadAsStringAsync();
Console.WriteLine("Response:");
Console.WriteLine(responseBody);
}
catch (HttpRequestException e)
{
Console.WriteLine($"Request Error: {e.Message}");
}
}
}
}
```

In this example, we create an instance of HttpClient, send a GET request to "https://api.example.com/data," and read the response as a string. Make sure to handle exceptions and check for successful responses using EnsureSuccessStatusCode.

Using Third-Party Libraries

While HttpClient is suitable for basic HTTP requests, you might encounter scenarios where third-party libraries can simplify consuming web APIs and handling JSON data. Popular libraries include:

- **Newtonsoft.Json:** This library provides powerful JSON serialization and deserialization capabilities. You can use it to easily convert JSON responses into C# objects and vice versa.

```
using Newtonsoft.Json;

// Deserialize JSON response to a C# object

MyDataObject dataObject =
JsonConvert.DeserializeObject<MyDataObject>(responseBody);
```

- **RestSharp:** RestSharp is a popular library that simplifies making RESTful API requests and handling responses.

```
using RestSharp;

// Create a RestClient instance

var client = new RestClient("https://api.example.com");

// Create a request and specify the resource

var request = new RestRequest("/data", Method.GET);

// Execute the request and handle the response

IRestResponse response = client.Execute(request);
```

```
string responseBody = response.Content;
```

Authentication and Headers

When working with web APIs, you may need to provide authentication tokens or set custom headers in your requests. You can do this with HttpClient by adding headers to the request:

```
using System.Net.Http.Headers;

// Create an HttpClient instance

using (HttpClient client = new HttpClient())

{

// Set authentication token in the request header

client.DefaultRequestHeaders.Authorization = new AuthenticationHeaderValue("Bearer", "your-token");

// Send the request and handle the response

HttpResponseMessage response = await client.GetAsync("https://api.example.com/data");

// ...

}
```

Conclusion

Consuming web APIs is a crucial part of modern software development, allowing your applications to interact with external services and retrieve data. In C#, you have various options for making HTTP requests, processing responses, and handling authentication. Choose the approach and libraries that best fit your project's requirements.

Section 8.5: Asynchronous Programming and Networking

Asynchronous programming is essential in C# for performing non-blocking operations, such as making network requests, to improve application responsiveness and scalability. In this section, we'll explore asynchronous programming in the context of networking.

Understanding Asynchronous Programming

Asynchronous programming allows you to execute multiple tasks concurrently without blocking the main thread. It's crucial for tasks that involve waiting for external resources like network data or file I/O. In C#, the async and await keywords simplify asynchronous code development.

Here's a basic example of an asynchronous method:

```
using System;

using System.Net.Http;

using System.Threading.Tasks;

class Program

{

static async Task Main()

{
```

```
// Create an HttpClient instance
using (HttpClient client = new HttpClient())
{
try
{
// Asynchronously send a GET request and await the response
HttpResponseMessage response = await client.GetAsync("https://api.example.com/data");
// Ensure a successful response
response.EnsureSuccessStatusCode();
// Asynchronously read the response content
string responseBody = await response.Content.ReadAsStringAsync();
// Process the response data
Console.WriteLine("Response:");
Console.WriteLine(responseBody);
}
catch (HttpRequestException e)
{
Console.WriteLine($"Request Error: {e.Message}");
}
```

```
}
}
}
```

In this example, the async and await keywords make it possible to perform non-blocking I/O operations while maintaining a responsive application.

Benefits of Asynchronous Programming in Networking

When working with networking tasks, asynchronous programming offers several advantages:

1. **Improved Responsiveness:** By not blocking the main thread, your application remains responsive, ensuring a smoother user experience.
2. **Efficient Resource Utilization:** Asynchronous operations allow you to efficiently utilize system resources, reducing the need for thread-blocking and context switching.
3. **Scalability:** Asynchronous code can handle a larger number of concurrent requests, making your application more scalable.

Asynchronous Web API Requests

When making web API requests, asynchronous methods are particularly valuable. C#'s HttpClient class provides asynchronous methods for making GET, POST, PUT, and DELETE requests, as demonstrated in the example above. You can also use asynchronous libraries like RestSharp to simplify network operations.

Task-Based Asynchronous Pattern (TAP)

In C#, asynchronous programming follows the Task-Based Asynchronous Pattern (TAP). Tasks represent asynchronous operations, and you can compose and await them to achieve concurrency and maintain a responsive application.

Error Handling in Asynchronous Code

Proper error handling is crucial in asynchronous code. Use try-catch blocks or propagate exceptions to ensure that your application gracefully handles errors that may occur during asynchronous operations.

In conclusion, asynchronous programming is vital when working with networking in C#. It allows your application to perform non-blocking operations, ensuring responsiveness and scalability. When making web API requests or dealing with any network-related tasks, embrace asynchronous programming to enhance your application's performance and user experience.

Chapter 9: Multithreading and Parallel Programming

Section 9.1: Understanding Threads and Thread Safety

Multithreading is a powerful concept in C# that enables the execution of multiple threads (smaller units of a process) concurrently. Each thread runs independently and can perform tasks simultaneously, making efficient use of multi-core processors. However, multithreading introduces challenges, including thread safety concerns that developers must address.

What are Threads?

A thread is the smallest unit of execution within a process. In a C# program, the main thread is created automatically when the application starts. Developers can also create additional threads to perform tasks concurrently. Threads share the same memory space within a process, allowing them to communicate and coordinate tasks.

Benefits of Multithreading

Multithreading offers several advantages:

1. **Improved Performance:** Multithreading can lead to better performance by utilizing available CPU cores effectively.
2. **Responsiveness:** It helps keep the application responsive by preventing long-running tasks from blocking the user interface (UI) thread.
3. **Parallel Processing:** Multithreading enables parallel

processing, which is essential for tasks like data processing, rendering, and network communication.

Thread Safety

When multiple threads access shared data or resources simultaneously, it can lead to race conditions, data corruption, or unexpected behavior. Ensuring thread safety is critical to avoid these issues. Here are some common techniques to achieve thread safety:

- **Locking:** Use locks, such as lock statements or Mutex, to synchronize access to shared resources. This prevents multiple threads from accessing the resource simultaneously.

```
private readonly object lockObject = new object();

public void ThreadSafeMethod()

{

lock (lockObject)

{

// Access and modify shared resources safely

}

}
```

- **Immutable Data:** Use immutable data structures whenever possible. Immutable objects cannot be modified after creation, making them inherently thread-safe.

- **Thread-Safe Collections:** C# provides thread-safe collections like ConcurrentDictionary, ConcurrentQueue, and ConcurrentStack that are designed for concurrent access.

```
using System.Collections.Concurrent;

// Create a thread-safe dictionary

ConcurrentDictionary<string, int> dictionary = new
ConcurrentDictionary<string, int>();

dictionary.TryAdd("Key", 42);
```

- **Avoid Shared State:** Minimize shared state between threads. When possible, design your application to work with independent data structures for each thread.

Thread Synchronization

Thread synchronization is essential for coordinating the execution of multiple threads. Synchronization primitives, such as Monitor, Semaphore, and AutoResetEvent, allow threads to wait for specific conditions before proceeding.

```
using System.Threading;

// Using a Mutex for synchronization

Mutex mutex = new Mutex();

void ThreadMethod()

{

mutex.WaitOne(); // Wait for access
```

```
// Perform thread-safe operations

mutex.ReleaseMutex(); // Release the mutex

}
```

Conclusion

Multithreading is a powerful technique for improving application performance and responsiveness. However, it introduces challenges related to thread safety. Understanding threads, thread safety principles, and synchronization mechanisms is crucial for developing robust multithreaded applications in C#.

Section 9.2: Creating Multithreaded Applications

In the previous section, we discussed the fundamentals of threads and thread safety. Now, let's explore how to create multithreaded applications in C#. Multithreading allows you to perform tasks concurrently, which is particularly valuable for improving the performance of CPU-bound or I/O-bound operations.

Creating Threads

C# provides several ways to create threads. One common approach is to use the Thread class from the System.Threading namespace. Here's a basic example of creating and starting a new thread:

```
using System;

using System.Threading;

class Program

{
```

```
static void Main()

{

// Create and start a new thread

Thread thread = new Thread(DoWork);

thread.Start();

// The main thread continues executing here

Console.WriteLine("Main thread is running.");

// Wait for the thread to complete

thread.Join();

}

static void DoWork()

{

// This method runs on a separate thread

Console.WriteLine("Worker thread is running.");

}

}
```

In this example, we create a new thread using the Thread class and specify the method (DoWork) that the thread should execute. The Start method begins the execution of the thread. The main thread continues running other tasks and waits for the worker thread to finish using Join.

Thread States

Threads in C# can be in various states, including:

- **Running:** The thread is actively executing code.
- **Suspended:** The thread is temporarily halted.
- **Aborted:** The thread is forcefully terminated.
- **Waiting:** The thread is waiting for a signal or event.
- **Dead:** The thread has finished execution.

Thread Priority

Threads can have different priorities, such as Lowest, BelowNormal, Normal, AboveNormal, and Highest. Priority affects how the operating system schedules threads for execution. However, it's essential to use priority judiciously, as it can impact system performance and fairness.

```
Thread thread = new Thread(DoWork);

thread.Priority = ThreadPriority.AboveNormal;
```

ThreadPool

The .NET Framework also provides a thread pool (ThreadPool) for managing and reusing threads efficiently. Instead of creating threads manually, you can queue tasks to the thread pool, which automatically manages thread creation and reuse.

```
ThreadPool.QueueUserWorkItem(DoWork);
```

Challenges of Multithreading

While multithreading offers benefits, it introduces complexities:

1. **Thread Safety:** Ensuring thread safety becomes critical when multiple threads access shared resources.
2. **Synchronization:** Coordinating the execution of threads and preventing race conditions requires careful synchronization.
3. **Debugging:** Debugging multithreaded applications can be challenging due to non-deterministic behavior.

In conclusion, creating multithreaded applications in C# can enhance performance and concurrency. However, it's essential to understand thread states, prioritize tasks appropriately, and address thread safety concerns to build robust and efficient multithreaded applications.

Section 9.3: Task Parallel Library (TPL) and Parallel LINQ

The Task Parallel Library (TPL) is a powerful framework in C# for simplifying multithreaded programming. It provides higher-level abstractions for managing and coordinating parallel tasks, making it easier to write efficient and scalable concurrent code.

Tasks and Task Parallelism

A Task in the TPL represents an asynchronous operation that can be executed concurrently. You can think of it as a unit of work that can run on a separate thread. Tasks abstract away low-level details of managing threads and allow you to focus on writing parallel code.

Here's a simple example of creating and running tasks:

```
using System;

using System.Threading.Tasks;

class Program

{

static async Task Main()

{

Task task1 = Task.Run(() => Console.WriteLine("Task 1 is running."));

Task task2 = Task.Run(() => Console.WriteLine("Task 2 is running."));

await Task.WhenAll(task1, task2);

Console.WriteLine("Both tasks have completed.");

}

}
```

In this example, we create two tasks using Task.Run. The await Task.WhenAll statement waits for both tasks to complete before proceeding. This allows efficient parallel execution of tasks without the need to manage threads explicitly.

Parallel LINQ (PLINQ)

Parallel LINQ (PLINQ) extends LINQ (Language-Integrated Query) to enable parallel processing of data. PLINQ automatically partitions data and processes it concurrently, improving the performance of operations like filtering, mapping, and aggregating large data sets.

Here's an example of using PLINQ to perform a parallel Select operation:

```
using System;

using System.Linq;

using System.Threading.Tasks;

class Program

{

static void Main()

{

int[] numbers = Enumerable.Range(1, 1000000).ToArray();

var result = numbers.AsParallel()

.Select(x => x * 2)

.ToArray();

Console.WriteLine($"Result count: {result.Length}");

}

}
```

In this example, the AsParallel extension method converts the numbers collection into a parallel query, and the Select operation is executed in parallel, potentially leveraging multiple CPU cores.

Benefits and Considerations

The TPL and PLINQ offer several advantages:

- **Simplified Parallelism:** TPL abstracts away many complexities of multithreading, making it easier to write parallel code.

- **Automatic Load Balancing:** TPL dynamically distributes tasks across available processors for efficient load balancing.

- **Cancellation and Exception Handling:** TPL provides mechanisms for canceling tasks and handling exceptions in a structured way.

However, it's essential to use parallelism judiciously. Not all operations benefit from parallelism, and excessive parallelism can lead to overhead and decreased performance.

In conclusion, the Task Parallel Library and Parallel LINQ are powerful tools for achieving parallelism in C# applications. They simplify the development of parallel code, improve performance, and provide features for managing concurrency effectively. When used appropriately, these tools can greatly enhance the scalability and responsiveness of your applications.

Section 9.4: Synchronization and Locking

In a multithreaded environment, multiple threads can access shared resources concurrently, leading to potential issues like data corruption or race conditions. Synchronization mechanisms are crucial to ensure that threads coordinate properly and access shared resources safely.

Race Conditions

A race condition occurs when multiple threads access and modify shared data concurrently, leading to unpredictable results. Consider the following example:

```
using System;

using System.Threading;

class Program

{

static int counter = 0;

static void Main()

{

Thread thread1 = new Thread(IncrementCounter);

Thread thread2 = new Thread(IncrementCounter);

thread1.Start();

thread2.Start();

thread1.Join();

thread2.Join();

Console.WriteLine($"Counter: {counter}");

}

static void IncrementCounter()

{
```

```
for (int i = 0; i < 100000; i++)
{
// Simulate a race condition
int temp = counter;
Thread.Sleep(1); // Simulate some work
counter = temp + 1;
}
}
}
```

In this example, two threads increment a shared counter variable. Without proper synchronization, the results can vary each time you run the program due to the race condition.

Locking with lock

One common synchronization mechanism in C# is the lock statement. It ensures that only one thread can access a specific section of code at a time. Here's how you can use it:

```
using System;
using System.Threading;
class Program
{
static int counter = 0;
static readonly object lockObject = new object();
```

```
static void Main()
{
Thread thread1 = new Thread(IncrementCounter);
Thread thread2 = new Thread(IncrementCounter);
thread1.Start();
thread2.Start();
thread1.Join();
thread2.Join();
Console.WriteLine($"Counter: {counter}");
}
static void IncrementCounter()
{
for (int i = 0; i < 100000; i++)
{
lock (lockObject)
{
int temp = counter;
Thread.Sleep(1); // Simulate some work
counter = temp + 1;
}
```

```
}
}
}
```

In this modified example, we use the lock statement to protect the critical section of code where counter is accessed. This ensures that only one thread can execute the critical section at any given time, preventing race conditions.

Deadlocks

While synchronization is essential, it can lead to deadlocks if not used carefully. A deadlock occurs when two or more threads are unable to proceed because each is waiting for a resource held by the other. To avoid deadlocks, it's crucial to follow best practices when acquiring locks and avoid circular dependencies.

Other Synchronization Constructs

Apart from lock, C# provides other synchronization constructs like Monitor, Mutex, Semaphore, and AutoResetEvent. The choice of synchronization mechanism depends on the specific requirements of your multithreaded application.

In conclusion, synchronization and locking are essential tools for ensuring thread safety in multithreaded C# applications. Properly synchronized code prevents race conditions and data corruption, making your applications more robust and reliable in concurrent scenarios. However, it's crucial to be aware of potential deadlocks and choose the appropriate synchronization mechanism for your specific needs.

Section 9.5: Dealing with Concurrency Issues

Concurrency issues are common in multithreaded applications. These issues can lead to unexpected behavior, crashes, or data corruption. Dealing with concurrency issues effectively is crucial for building reliable software. In this section, we'll explore some common concurrency issues and how to address them.

1. Race Conditions

Race conditions occur when multiple threads access shared data simultaneously, leading to unpredictable results. To mitigate race conditions, you can use synchronization mechanisms like lock to ensure that only one thread can access critical sections of code at a time. This prevents data corruption and maintains the integrity of shared resources.

Here's a simple example using lock:

```
object lockObject = new object();

int sharedData = 0;

void IncrementSharedData()

{

lock (lockObject)

{

sharedData++;

}

}
```

2. Deadlocks

Deadlocks happen when two or more threads are blocked, each waiting for a resource held by the other. To prevent deadlocks, follow best practices when acquiring locks and avoid circular dependencies. You can also use timeouts or other strategies to detect and recover from deadlocks.

3. Thread-Safety

Ensuring thread-safety is crucial to prevent data corruption and maintain application stability. Avoid shared mutable state when possible, use immutable objects, and employ synchronization constructs when working with shared resources.

4. Atomic Operations

Atomic operations are operations that execute as a single, uninterruptible unit. In C#, you can use the Interlocked class for atomic operations on numeric types and volatile for ensuring memory visibility between threads.

```
int sharedCounter = 0;

void IncrementCounterSafely()

{

Interlocked.Increment(ref sharedCounter);

}
```

5. Testing and Debugging

Thoroughly test your multithreaded code to uncover concurrency issues. Tools like Visual Studio's Parallel Stacks and Concurrency

Visualizer can help identify problems. Additionally, consider using unit tests and stress tests to verify your code's correctness under various concurrency scenarios.

6. Asynchronous Programming

Asynchronous programming using async and await can simplify concurrency management by allowing your application to remain responsive while performing I/O-bound or CPU-bound tasks asynchronously. This can improve overall application performance and responsiveness.

```
async Task<string> FetchDataAsync()
{
// Perform asynchronous I/O-bound operation
return await HttpClient.GetStringAsync("https://example.com/data");
}
```

7. Design for Concurrency

When designing your software architecture, consider concurrency from the beginning. Use design patterns like the Producer-Consumer pattern or the Actor model to simplify concurrency management and improve scalability.

In summary, dealing with concurrency issues is essential for building robust multithreaded applications. By understanding and addressing common issues like race conditions, deadlocks, and thread-safety, you can create software that performs well and provides a reliable user experience, even in highly concurrent environments.

Chapter 10: Advanced Topics in C

Section 10.1: Dynamic Programming and ExpandoObject

In this section, we'll delve into dynamic programming and the ExpandoObject in C#. These topics offer flexibility and power in scenarios where you need to work with data structures that can change at runtime or when dealing with dynamic data sources.

Dynamic Programming

Dynamic programming is a programming technique used to solve problems by breaking them down into smaller subproblems and storing the results of those subproblems to avoid redundant calculations. While it's not unique to C#, C# provides support for dynamic programming through data structures like dictionaries and memoization.

Consider the Fibonacci sequence as an example:

```
Dictionary<int, long> memo = new Dictionary<int, long>();

long Fibonacci(int n)

{

if (n <= 1)

return n;

if (memo.TryGetValue(n, out long result))

return result;

result = Fibonacci(n - 1) + Fibonacci(n - 2);
```

```
memo[n] = result;

return result;

}
```

Here, we use a dictionary (memo) to store previously computed Fibonacci numbers, avoiding redundant calculations.

ExpandoObject

ExpandoObject is a dynamic object that allows you to add properties and methods to it at runtime. This can be incredibly useful when working with data from sources like JSON or when you need to create dynamic objects without defining a formal class.

```
dynamic person = new ExpandoObject();

person.Name = "John";

person.Age = 30;

Console.WriteLine($"Name: {person.Name}, Age: {person.Age}");
```

You can also add methods to an ExpandoObject:

```
person.SayHello = new Action(() => Console.WriteLine("Hello, I'm " + person.Name));

person.SayHello(); // Calls the dynamically added method
```

This flexibility makes ExpandoObject a valuable tool when dealing with data structures that may not have a fixed schema.

Use Cases

Dynamic programming is often used in algorithmic problem-solving to optimize recursive solutions, while ExpandoObject is handy when dealing with loosely structured data or when creating ad-hoc objects. Both techniques provide flexibility and power when you need to work with dynamic data in C#.

In this section, we've explored the concepts of dynamic programming and ExpandoObject and provided examples of how they can be applied in C#. These advanced topics expand your toolkit and enable you to tackle a wider range of programming challenges.

Section 10.2: Reflection and Attributes

In this section, we will explore reflection and attributes in C#. Reflection allows you to inspect and interact with the metadata of types, methods, and other program entities at runtime. Attributes, on the other hand, are a way to add metadata or declarative information to your code elements.

Reflection

Reflection provides the ability to examine the metadata of types and objects at runtime. This metadata includes information about methods, properties, fields, and more. Reflection is often used in scenarios such as:

- Loading and interacting with assemblies dynamically.
- Creating instances of types that are not known at compile time.
- Enumerating and invoking methods or properties of objects based on their metadata.

Here's a basic example of how to use reflection to get information about a type:

```
using System;

using System.Reflection;

class Program

{

static void Main()

{

Type type = typeof(string);

Console.WriteLine("Type Name: " + type.Name);

Console.WriteLine("Full Name: " + type.FullName);

Console.WriteLine("Assembly Qualified Name: " + type.AssemblyQualifiedName);

foreach (MethodInfo method in type.GetMethods())

{

Console.WriteLine("Method: " + method.Name);

}

}

}
```

Attributes

Attributes in C# are declarative tags that can be applied to various program entities. They provide additional information about the entities they tag. Attributes are often used for:

- Adding metadata to code elements (e.g., classes, methods, properties).
- Controlling code generation (e.g., serialization, code analysis).
- Enabling runtime behavior (e.g., custom validation, security checks).

Here's an example of defining and using a custom attribute:

```
using System;

[AttributeUsage(AttributeTargets.Class |
AttributeTargets.Method)]

public class MyCustomAttribute : Attribute

{

public string Description { get; }

public MyCustomAttribute(string description)

{

Description = description;

}

}
```

```
[MyCustom("This is a custom attribute")]
class MyClass
{
[MyCustom("This is a custom method attribute")]
public void MyMethod() { }
}
```

In this example, we define a custom attribute MyCustomAttribute that can be applied to classes and methods. We then use this attribute to add metadata to MyClass and its MyMethod.

Use Cases

Reflection and attributes are powerful tools in C# that enable dynamic behavior and metadata-driven programming. Reflection is especially useful in scenarios where you need to work with types and objects at runtime, while attributes allow you to add custom metadata to your code for various purposes, including code generation and runtime behavior control.

Section 10.3: Interoperability with Native Code

Interoperability between C# and native code (code written in languages like C and C++) allows you to leverage existing native libraries and functionalities in your C# applications. This is particularly useful when you want to reuse legacy code, interact with platform-specific APIs, or access hardware resources directly. In this section, we'll explore different techniques and tools for achieving interoperability between C# and native code.

P/Invoke (Platform Invocation Services)

Platform Invocation Services, often referred to as P/Invoke, is a feature in C# that allows you to call functions defined in native libraries (DLLs) from managed C# code. P/Invoke relies on the DllImport attribute to declare the signature of the native function and its library. Here's an example:

```
using System;

using System.Runtime.InteropServices;

class Program

{

[DllImport("user32.dll")]

public static extern int MessageBox(IntPtr hWnd, string text, string caption, uint type);

static void Main()

{

MessageBox(IntPtr.Zero, "Hello from P/Invoke!", "Message Box", 0);

}

}
```

In this example, we use P/Invoke to call the MessageBox function from the user32.dll library, displaying a message box.

COM Interop (Component Object Model Interoperability)

COM Interop enables C# applications to interact with COM objects, which are often used in Windows development. You can use COM Interop to access functionality exposed by COM components, such as Microsoft Office applications or third-party COM libraries. C# provides a way to generate interop assemblies (runtime-callable wrappers) from COM type libraries.

C++ Interop

When you need to interact with C++ code from C#, you can use C++ Interop techniques. One common approach is to create a C++/CLI wrapper that acts as an intermediary between C# and native C++ code. C++/CLI allows you to write managed code that can call native C++ functions and use native C++ data types.

.NET Core and .NET 5+ Support

Interoperability with native code is not limited to the Windows platform. .NET Core and .NET 5+ have expanded support for cross-platform native interop. You can use P/Invoke and other techniques to work with native libraries on different operating systems, including Linux and macOS.

Use Cases

Interoperability with native code is essential when developing applications that require access to platform-specific features or when integrating with existing native libraries. Common use cases include:

- Accessing Windows APIs for system-level tasks.

- Integrating with third-party libraries written in C or C++.
- Reusing legacy code written in native languages.
- Accessing hardware resources directly through device drivers.

When working with native code, it's crucial to ensure proper memory management, handle exceptions, and consider platform-specific differences to maintain application stability and portability.

Section 10.4: Advanced Debugging Techniques

Debugging is an essential part of software development, and C# provides a robust set of tools and techniques to help you identify and resolve issues in your code. In this section, we'll explore some advanced debugging techniques that can assist you in tracking down complex bugs and improving your overall debugging process.

Conditional Breakpoints

Conditional breakpoints allow you to break into the debugger only when specific conditions are met. Instead of stopping at every iteration or function call, you can set conditions that filter when the breakpoint should trigger. To use conditional breakpoints in Visual Studio, right-click on a breakpoint and set its conditions based on variables or expressions.

```
int[] numbers = { 1, 2, 3, 4, 5 };

foreach (int number in numbers)
```

```
{
if (number % 2 == 0)
{
Console.WriteLine(number);
}
}
```

In this example, you can set a conditional breakpoint to break when number % 2 == 0, allowing you to inspect the variables only when the condition is true.

Tracepoints

Tracepoints are like print statements but within your debugging environment. Instead of adding Console.WriteLine statements for debugging and then removing them later, you can insert tracepoints in Visual Studio. These tracepoints output messages to the debug output window without modifying your code.

DebuggerDisplay Attribute

The DebuggerDisplay attribute allows you to specify how an object should be displayed in the debugger. You can customize how objects are shown in the debugger windows, making it easier to inspect complex data structures.

```
[DebuggerDisplay("Name: {Name}, Age: {Age}")]
class Person
{
```

```
public string Name { get; set; }

public int Age { get; set; }

}
```

In this example, when you inspect an instance of the Person class in the debugger, it will display the name and age properties as specified in the DebuggerDisplay attribute.

DebuggerStepThrough Attribute

Sometimes, you may have code that you don't want to step through while debugging. You can use the DebuggerStepThrough attribute on methods to tell the debugger to skip over them.

```
[DebuggerStepThrough]

public void SomeMethod()

{

// Debugger will skip this method when stepping through

}
```

Advanced Breakpoint Features

Modern IDEs like Visual Studio offer advanced breakpoint features, such as data breakpoints (breaking when a variable's value changes), hit counts (breaking after a certain number of hits), and breakpoint filters (breaking only when specific conditions are met).

These advanced debugging techniques can significantly improve your productivity and efficiency when identifying and fixing issues in your C# code. Understanding how to use these tools effectively is an essential skill for any developer.

Section 10.5: C# Best Practices and Performance Optimization

In this section, we will explore some best practices and techniques for optimizing the performance of your C# applications. Efficient code not only improves the user experience but also reduces resource consumption and operational costs.

1. Use StringBuilder for String Concatenation

When you need to concatenate strings in a loop or a series of operations, use the StringBuilder class instead of the + operator. StringBuilder is more efficient for building strings because it avoids the creation of unnecessary intermediate string objects.

```
StringBuilder stringBuilder = new StringBuilder();

for (int i = 0; i < 10000; i++)

{

stringBuilder.Append(i.ToString());

}

string result = stringBuilder.ToString();
```

2. Avoid Using Exceptions for Flow Control

Exceptions should not be used for regular flow control. They are intended for handling exceptional situations. Using exceptions for regular control flow can lead to performance issues.

```
// Avoid this

try
```

```
{
int result = int.Parse(input);
}
catch (FormatException)
{
// Handle the error
}
// Instead, use TryParse
if (int.TryParse(input, out int result))
{
// Use the result
}
else
{
// Handle the error
}
```

3. Dispose of Resources Properly

Ensure that objects that implement IDisposable, such as file streams or database connections, are properly disposed of when they are no longer needed. You can use the using statement to automatically dispose of these resources when they go out of scope.

```
using (FileStream fileStream = new FileStream("data.txt", FileMode.Open))
{
// Read or write data
} // fileStream is automatically disposed here
```

4. Optimize Database Access

When working with databases, minimize the number of queries and use appropriate indexing to improve query performance. Consider using an Object-Relational Mapping (ORM) framework like Entity Framework for efficient database access.

```
// Avoid N+1 query problem
var customers = dbContext.Customers.Include(c => c.Orders).ToList();
```

5. Profile and Measure Performance

Use profiling tools and performance counters to identify bottlenecks in your application. Profiling can help you pinpoint areas that need optimization, whether it's CPU-bound or memory-bound performance issues.

6. Use Asynchronous Programming

For I/O-bound operations, use asynchronous programming with the async and await keywords. Asynchronous code can improve the responsiveness of your application by allowing it to continue processing other tasks while waiting for I/O operations to complete.

```
public async Task DownloadDataAsync()
```

```
{
HttpClient httpClient = new HttpClient();
string data = await httpClient.GetStringAsync("https://example.com/data");
// Process data
}
```

7. Minimize Garbage Collection

Excessive garbage collection can impact application performance. Try to minimize the creation of short-lived objects and use object pooling for frequently used objects.

```
// Object pooling example
ObjectPool<StringBuilder> pool = new ObjectPool<StringBuilder>(() => new StringBuilder(), 100);
StringBuilder sb = pool.GetObject();
sb.Append("Some text");
pool.PutObject(sb); // Return to the pool when done
```

These best practices and optimization techniques can help you build high-performance C# applications that are responsive and efficient. Always remember that performance optimization should be guided by profiling and testing to ensure that improvements are made where they matter most.

Chapter 11: Building Desktop Applications with WPF

Section 11.1: Introduction to Windows Presentation Foundation (WPF)

Windows Presentation Foundation (WPF) is a powerful and flexible framework for building desktop applications on the Windows operating system. It provides a rich set of tools and libraries for creating modern, visually appealing, and interactive user interfaces. WPF is a part of the .NET ecosystem and is commonly used for developing Windows applications, including business software, multimedia applications, and games.

Key Features of WPF

WPF offers several key features that make it a popular choice for desktop application development:

1. **XAML (eXtensible Application Markup Language)**: WPF uses XAML for designing user interfaces. XAML is a markup language that allows you to define the layout, controls, and styles of your application's user interface in a declarative manner. This separation of UI from code simplifies design and development collaboration.
2. **Data Binding**: WPF provides robust data binding capabilities, allowing you to easily bind UI elements to data sources. This enables automatic synchronization of data between the user interface and the underlying data model, reducing the need for manual updates.
3. **Styles and Templates**: WPF allows you to define styles and templates for UI controls. Styles enable consistent

visual appearance, while templates allow you to customize the structure of controls. This flexibility helps create unique and visually appealing interfaces.

4. **Vector Graphics and Resolution Independence**: WPF uses vector graphics for rendering, which ensures that your application looks sharp on screens with different resolutions and sizes. This makes it suitable for a variety of devices, from traditional desktop monitors to high-DPI displays.
5. **Animation and Multimedia**: WPF supports rich animations and multimedia capabilities. You can create smooth animations and integrate audio and video elements into your applications.
6. **Custom Controls**: You can create custom controls and user interface elements tailored to your application's specific requirements. This extensibility allows for greater creativity and adaptability.

WPF Application Structure

A typical WPF application consists of the following components:

- **MainWindow**: The main window of the application, which hosts the user interface elements.

- **XAML Files**: These files define the layout and appearance of the user interface using XAML markup.

- **Code-Behind**: The C# or VB.NET code associated with the XAML files. This code handles user interactions and application logic.

- **Resources**: Resources such as styles, templates, and images that are used to enhance the user interface.

- **ViewModels**: In MVVM (Model-View-ViewModel) pattern-based applications, view models represent the application's logic and data.

MVVM Pattern in WPF

Many WPF applications follow the MVVM architectural pattern, which promotes separation of concerns. In MVVM:

- **Model**: Represents the application's data and business logic.

- **View**: Defines the user interface and is created using XAML.

- **ViewModel**: Acts as an intermediary between the View and Model, providing data-binding capabilities and handling user interactions.

Getting Started with WPF

To start building WPF applications, you'll need Visual Studio or a compatible IDE. Visual Studio provides templates for creating WPF projects and a design surface for designing your user interface with XAML.

In the upcoming sections, we'll explore various aspects of WPF development, including creating WPF windows and controls, data binding, styling, and implementing the MVVM pattern.

WPF offers a modern and versatile platform for desktop application development, allowing you to create Windows applications with rich and interactive user interfaces. Whether you're building business applications or multimedia experiences, WPF provides the tools and flexibility you need to bring your ideas to life.

Section 11.2: Creating WPF Windows and Controls

In Windows Presentation Foundation (WPF), creating windows and controls is a fundamental aspect of designing your application's user interface. WPF provides a wide range of built-in controls that you can use to build sophisticated desktop applications. In this section, we'll explore how to create WPF windows and work with common controls.

Creating a WPF Window

A WPF window is the primary container for hosting user interface elements. To create a WPF window, you typically follow these steps:

1. Open your WPF project in Visual Studio or your preferred IDE.
2. Open the XAML file associated with your window. By convention, the main window of a WPF application is named MainWindow.xaml.
3. In the XAML file, define the layout and content of your window using XAML markup. For example, a simple window definition might look like this:

```
<Window x:Class="YourNamespace.MainWindow"

xmlns="http://schemas.microsoft.com/winfx/2006/
xaml/presentation"

xmlns:x="http://schemas.microsoft.com/winfx/2006/
xaml"

Title="My WPF Window" Width="400"
Height="300">
```

<!—Add your user interface controls here—>

</Window>

This code creates a window titled "My WPF Window" with a width of 400 pixels and a height of 300 pixels.

1. Inside the <Window> element, you can add various controls, such as buttons, text boxes, labels, and more. These controls define the visual elements and user interaction for your application.

Common WPF Controls

WPF provides a rich set of controls that you can use to build your application's user interface. Here are some common controls:

- **Button**: Represents a clickable button that performs an action when clicked.
- **TextBlock**: Displays text in a read-only format.
- **TextBox**: Allows users to input and edit text.
- **Label**: Displays a text label for other controls.
- **RadioButton**: Represents a choice in a group of options where only one option can be selected.
- **CheckBox**: Represents a binary choice that can be selected or deselected.
- **ComboBox**: Provides a dropdown list of items for selection.

- **ListView**: Displays a list of items in a grid format.
- **ListBox**: Displays a list of items in a vertical list.
- **Menu**: Defines a menu structure for the application.
- **TabControl**: Organizes content into tabbed pages.

Adding Controls to a Window

To add controls to a WPF window, you can simply insert them within the <Window> element in your XAML file. Here's an example of adding a Button and a TextBox to a window:

```
<Window x:Class="YourNamespace.MainWindow"

xmlns="http://schemas.microsoft.com/winfx/2006/xaml/presentation"

xmlns:x="http://schemas.microsoft.com/winfx/2006/xaml"

Title="My WPF Window" Width="400" Height="300">

<Grid>

<Button Content="Click Me" Width="100" Height="30" />

<TextBox Width="200" Height="30" Margin="120,50,0,0" />

</Grid>

</Window>
```

In this example, a Button with the text “Click Me” and a TextBox are added to the window within a Grid layout container. The Width, Height, and Margin properties define the size and position of the controls.

Running Your WPF Application

To run your WPF application and see the window with its controls, set your main window as the startup object in your project settings. Then, simply build and run the application.

WPF provides a powerful and flexible way to create desktop applications with rich user interfaces. By understanding how to create windows and work with common controls, you can start building the foundation of your WPF application's user interface.

Section 11.3: Data Binding in WPF

Data binding is a fundamental concept in Windows Presentation Foundation (WPF) that allows you to establish a connection between the user interface (UI) elements in your application and the underlying data. This powerful feature simplifies the process of displaying and updating data within your WPF application. In this section, we'll explore data binding and how to use it effectively in WPF.

Understanding Data Binding

At its core, data binding is about synchronizing the data in your application with the visual elements in the UI. It allows you to establish a connection between a property or data source and a UI control, such as a text box, label, or list view. When the data changes, the UI control automatically reflects those changes, and vice versa.

Data binding is particularly useful in scenarios where you have a collection of data items (e.g., a list of items retrieved from a database) and you want to display them in a user-friendly way without manually updating the UI.

Data Binding Modes

WPF supports different data binding modes that determine how data is transferred between the source and the target UI element. The most common data binding modes are:

1. **OneWay**: In this mode, data flows from the source (e.g., a property) to the target (e.g., a UI control), but changes in the target do not affect the source. It's a read-only binding.
2. **TwoWay**: This mode enables bidirectional data binding. Changes in the source are reflected in the target, and changes in the target are also propagated back to the source.
3. **OneTime**: Data is transferred from the source to the target only once when the binding is initially established. Further changes in the source are not reflected in the target.
4. **OneWayToSource**: Similar to OneWay, data flows from the target to the source. Changes in the target are reflected in the source, but not the other way around.

Data Binding Syntax

In WPF, you can define data bindings in XAML using a concise and expressive syntax. Here's a basic example of data binding for a TextBlock control:

```
<TextBlock Text="{Binding UserName}" />
```

In this example, the Text property of the TextBlock is bound to the UserName property of the data source. Whenever the UserName property changes, the text displayed in the TextBlock will automatically update.

DataContext and Binding Context

To enable data binding, you typically set the DataContext property of a UI element to an object that provides the data. For example, you might set the DataContext of a window to an instance of a view model class. The UI controls within that window can then bind to properties of the view model.

Data Binding with Collections

Data binding is particularly powerful when working with collections, such as lists or arrays of data. You can bind a UI control, like a ListBox or a DataGrid, to a collection and have it automatically display the items in the collection.

```
<ListBox ItemsSource="{Binding Students}"
DisplayMemberPath="Name" />
```

In this example, the ListBox is bound to a collection of students, and it displays the names of the students. Any changes in the Students collection are automatically reflected in the ListBox.

Implementing INotifyPropertyChanged

For data binding to work effectively, the data source objects should implement the INotifyPropertyChanged interface. This interface allows objects to notify the UI when a property value changes so that the UI can update accordingly.

```
public class Student : INotifyPropertyChanged

{

private string name;

public string Name
```

```
{
get { return name; }
set
{
if (name != value)
{
name = value;
OnPropertyChanged(nameof(Name));
}
}
}
public event PropertyChangedEventHandler PropertyChanged;
protected virtual void OnPropertyChanged(string propertyName)
{
PropertyChanged?.Invoke(this, new
PropertyChangedEventArgs(propertyName));
}
}
```

In this example, the Student class implements INotifyPropertyChanged, and the Name property invokes the OnPropertyChanged method when its value changes.

Data Binding in Code-Behind

While data binding in XAML is common, you can also establish data bindings in code-behind (C#) if necessary. This gives you more flexibility in dynamically creating and configuring bindings.

```
Binding binding = new Binding("UserName")

{

Source = user,

Mode = BindingMode.OneWay

};

textBlock.SetBinding(TextBlock.TextProperty, binding);
```

Here, a Binding object is created in code-behind, specifying the source (user object), the property to bind (UserName), and the binding mode (OneWay). Then, the binding is applied to the TextBlock control using the SetBinding method.

Summary

Data binding is a key feature of WPF that simplifies the synchronization of data between your application's logic

Section 11.4: Styling and Templating in WPF

Styling and templating are essential aspects of Windows Presentation Foundation (WPF) that allow you to customize the appearance and behavior of your WPF applications. In this section, we'll explore how you can use styles and templates to create visually appealing and consistent user interfaces.

Understanding Styles

A style in WPF is a collection of property settings that can be applied to multiple UI elements to achieve a uniform appearance. Styles promote consistency across your application's user interface by defining a set of common property values.

Here's an example of defining a style for all buttons in XAML:

```
<Style TargetType="Button">

<Setter Property="Background" Value="LightBlue" />

<Setter Property="Foreground" Value="White" />

<Setter Property="FontWeight" Value="Bold" />

</Style>
```

In this code, we define a style targeting the Button type. We set properties like Background, Foreground, and FontWeight to create a consistent look for all buttons in the application. To apply this style to a button, you simply reference it in the button's Style property.

Applying Styles

You can apply a style to an individual element by setting the Style property of that element. For example:

```
<Button Content="Submit" Style="{StaticResource MyButtonStyle}" />
```

In this case, the button is styled using the MyButtonStyle defined earlier.

Templating Controls

Templates in WPF allow you to redefine the structure and appearance of a control. This is especially useful when you need to create custom controls or radically change the look of standard controls. WPF provides two types of templates: control templates and data templates.

Control Templates

A control template defines the visual structure of a custom control. You can completely redesign how a control looks by providing a new template. Here's an example of defining a custom Button template:

```
<ControlTemplate x:Key="MyButtonTemplate"
TargetType="Button">

<Border Background="LightBlue">

<ContentPresenter />

</Border>

</ControlTemplate>
```

This template replaces the default appearance of a button with a simple Border containing the button's content.

Data Templates

Data templates are used to define how data objects are displayed in controls like ListBox, ListView, or ItemsControl. They allow you to control the layout of each item in a collection. Here's an example of a data template for a ListBox:

```
<ListBox ItemsSource="{Binding Students}">
<ListBox.ItemTemplate>
<DataTemplate>
<StackPanel Orientation="Horizontal">
<Image Source="{Binding ImageUrl}" Width="40" Height="40"
/>
<TextBlock Text="{Binding Name}" Margin="10,0,0,0" />
</StackPanel>
</DataTemplate>
</ListBox.ItemTemplate>
</ListBox>
```

In this example, the data template specifies how each student item should be displayed within the ListBox.

Reusing Styles and Templates

To maintain consistency and improve code organization, you can define styles and templates in resource dictionaries and reuse them throughout your application. This allows you to apply the same style or template to multiple elements easily.

Dynamic Styling

WPF also supports dynamic styling and theming. You can change styles and templates at runtime based on user preferences or application states, providing a more flexible user interface.

Summary

Styling and templating in WPF enable you to create visually appealing and consistent user interfaces. Styles help you define a common look and feel for your controls, while templates allow you to customize the visual structure of controls and data items. These features are powerful tools for creating modern and engaging WPF applications.

Section 11.5: MVVM Pattern in WPF

The Model-View-ViewModel (MVVM) pattern is a widely-used architectural pattern in Windows Presentation Foundation (WPF) development. It provides a structured way to separate the concerns of your application and achieve a clean separation of user interface (UI) logic from business logic. In this section, we will explore the MVVM pattern and how it can be applied in WPF applications.

Understanding the MVVM Pattern

MVVM consists of three main components:

1. **Model**: The Model represents the data and business logic of your application. It encapsulates the application's data and defines the rules and operations that can be performed on that data.
2. **View**: The View represents the user interface (UI) of your application. It is responsible for presenting data to the user and receiving user input. In WPF, the View is typically defined using XAML.
3. **ViewModel**: The ViewModel acts as an intermediary between the Model and the View. It exposes the data and operations required by the View and ensures that the View and Model remain independent of each other. The

ViewModel is responsible for data binding, handling user interactions, and updating the Model.

Key Principles of MVVM

Data Binding

One of the core principles of MVVM is data binding. WPF provides powerful data binding capabilities that allow you to establish a connection between the ViewModel and the View. Data binding ensures that changes in the ViewModel are automatically reflected in the View and vice versa.

Commands

In MVVM, user interactions are handled using commands. Commands are objects that encapsulate actions or operations that can be triggered from the View. Commands allow you to implement user interactions in a way that is decoupled from the UI, making it easier to test and maintain your application.

Dependency Injection

MVVM encourages the use of dependency injection to provide the ViewModel with the necessary dependencies, such as services and repositories. Dependency injection promotes the separation of concerns and testability of your application.

Creating a ViewModel

Here's a simplified example of creating a ViewModel for a list of students:

```
public class StudentViewModel : INotifyPropertyChanged

{

private ObservableCollection<Student> students;

public ObservableCollection<Student> Students

{

get { return students; }

set

{

students = value;

OnPropertyChanged(nameof(Students));

}

}

public StudentViewModel()

{

// Initialize the ObservableCollection and load data from the Model.

Students = new ObservableCollection<Student>(DataService.GetStudents());

}

// Implementation of INotifyPropertyChanged for two-way data binding.

public event PropertyChangedEventHandler PropertyChanged;
```

```
protected virtual void OnPropertyChanged(string propertyName)

{

PropertyChanged?.Invoke(this, new PropertyChangedEventArgs(propertyName));

}

}
```

In this example, the StudentViewModel exposes a collection of students (Students) and initializes it with data from the Model. It also implements the INotifyPropertyChanged interface to notify the View of property changes.

Binding the View

In the View (defined in XAML), you can bind to properties and commands defined in the ViewModel. Here's a snippet of XAML demonstrating data binding:

```
<ListBox ItemsSource="{Binding Students}">

<ListBox.ItemTemplate>

<DataTemplate>

<TextBlock Text="{Binding Name}" />

</DataTemplate>

</ListBox.ItemTemplate>

</ListBox>
```

In this XAML, the ItemsSource of the ListBox is bound to the Students property of the ViewModel, and the Text property of the TextBlock is bound to the Name property of each student.

Benefits of MVVM

The MVVM pattern offers several advantages:

- **Separation of Concerns**: MVVM enforces a clear separation of concerns between the Model, View, and ViewModel, making your application more maintainable and testable.

- **Testability**: Because the ViewModel contains the application's logic independently of the View, it becomes easier to write unit tests for the ViewModel.

- **Flexibility**: MVVM allows for greater flexibility in UI design and promotes code reuse through ViewModels.

- **Collaborative Development**: Multiple developers can work simultaneously on the View and ViewModel, promoting collaborative development.

Conclusion

The MVVM pattern is a powerful architectural pattern for developing WPF applications. It promotes separation of concerns, testability, and maintainability, making it a popular choice for building modern and robust Windows applications. When used effectively, MVVM can simplify the development process and enhance the overall quality of your WPF applications.

Chapter 12: Cross-Platform Mobile App

Development with Flutter

Flutter is an open-source UI software development toolkit created by Google. It is used for building natively compiled applications for mobile, web, and desktop from a single codebase. In this chapter, we will explore the fundamentals of Flutter and how to get started with mobile app development using this versatile framework.

Section 12.1: Getting Started with Flutter and Dart

Flutter uses the Dart programming language, which is also developed by Google. Dart is known for its speed, productivity, and ability to build high-quality applications. Before diving into Flutter, let's first set up the development environment and understand the basics of Dart.

Installing Flutter

To begin working with Flutter, follow these steps to install it on your system:

1. Visit the Flutter website[1] and download the Flutter SDK for your operating system.
2. Extract the downloaded archive to a location on your computer.
3. Add the Flutter bin directory to your system's PATH environment variable. This allows you to run Flutter commands from any terminal window.
4. Open a terminal and run flutter doctor. This command will check your system for any missing dependencies or configurations needed for Flutter development. Follow the instructions to resolve any issues.

---

1. https://flutter.dev/

Creating Your First Flutter App

Now that you have Flutter installed, let's create a simple Flutter app. Flutter uses a declarative syntax for building user interfaces, and it provides a rich set of widgets for constructing the UI.

1. Open a terminal and navigate to the directory where you want to create your Flutter project.
2. Run the following command to create a new Flutter app:

```
flutter create my_first_flutter_app
```

Replace my_first_flutter_app with your preferred project name.

1. Once the project is created, navigate to the project directory:

```
cd my_first_flutter_app
```

1. To open the project in your preferred code editor, run:

```
code .
```

Replace code with the appropriate command for your code editor.

Understanding Dart Basics

Before diving into Flutter's widgets and UI development, it's essential to grasp some Dart fundamentals. Dart is a modern, object-oriented language with features like strong typing and asynchronous programming.

Here's a brief example of Dart code:

```
void main() {
print('Hello, Dart!');
int sum(int a, int b) {
return a + b;
}
print('The sum of 3 and 4 is ${sum(3, 4)}.');
}
```

In this example:

- We define a main function as the entry point of the Dart program.
- Inside the main function, we declare a sum function that takes two integers as parameters and returns their sum.
- We use string interpolation to display the result of the sum function.

Running Your Flutter App

To run your Flutter app, ensure that you have an emulator or a physical device connected to your development environment. Then, execute the following command in the project directory:

```
flutter run
```

Flutter will compile and launch your app on the connected device. You should see your app's default interface on the screen.

Conclusion

In this section, we've taken the first steps in getting started with Flutter and Dart. You've learned how to set up the development environment, create a Flutter project, and run a simple Flutter app. As you continue your journey with Flutter, you'll explore its powerful widget-based UI development and build cross-platform mobile applications with ease.

Section 12.2: Building Flutter UI Components

Flutter's strength lies in its ability to create beautiful and highly customizable user interfaces (UIs) using a wide variety of widgets. In this section, we'll explore some of the essential Flutter widgets and learn how to build UI components for your mobile apps.

Understanding Flutter Widgets

Widgets are the building blocks of a Flutter app's UI. They are lightweight, self-contained elements that can represent anything from a button to a complete screen. Flutter provides a vast library of built-in widgets, making it easy to create complex UIs.

Stateless Widgets vs. Stateful Widgets

Flutter widgets fall into two categories: stateless and stateful.

- **Stateless widgets** are immutable, meaning their properties cannot change once they are created. They are ideal for representing UI elements that do not change over time.

- **Stateful widgets**, on the other hand, can change and update their properties. They are used for UI elements that need to respond to user interactions or other dynamic events.

Creating a Simple Flutter Widget

Let's create a basic Flutter widget to illustrate the concept:

```
import 'package:flutter/material.dart';

class MyWidget extends StatelessWidget {

@override

Widget build(BuildContext context) {

return Container(

color: Colors.blue,

child: Center(

child: Text(

'Hello, Flutter!',

style: TextStyle(

fontSize: 24,

color: Colors.white,

),

),

),
```

```
);
}
}
```

In this example:

- We import the flutter/material.dart library, which provides the core Flutter widgets.
- We create a custom stateless widget called MyWidget that returns a Container with a blue background and centered text.
- Inside the Container, we use the Center widget to center the Text widget that displays "Hello, Flutter!" with specified styling.

Using Your Custom Widget

Now that you've created a custom widget, you can use it within your Flutter app. For example, you can include MyWidget in the build method of your app's main widget:

```
void main() {
runApp(MyApp());
}
class MyApp extends StatelessWidget {
@override
Widget build(BuildContext context) {
```

```
return MaterialApp(
home: Scaffold(
appBar: AppBar(
title: Text('My Flutter App'),
),
body: MyWidget(), // Using our custom widget
),
);
}
}
```

In this example:

- The MyApp widget serves as the root widget of your Flutter app.
- Inside the Scaffold widget, we use MyWidget() to insert your custom widget into the app's UI.

Conclusion

Flutter's extensive widget library empowers you to create intricate and visually appealing UI components for your mobile applications. Understanding the difference between stateless and stateful widgets is crucial, as it determines how your UI elements behave in response to changes. In the next sections, we'll delve deeper into handling user interactions and managing the state of your Flutter apps.

Section 12.3: Navigating and Managing State in Flutter

Flutter's versatility extends to navigation and state management, critical aspects of mobile app development. In this section, we'll explore how to navigate between screens and manage the state of your Flutter application.

Navigation in Flutter

Navigation involves moving between different screens or "routes" within your Flutter app. Flutter provides a built-in mechanism for handling navigation through the use of navigators and routes.

Pushing and Popping Routes

- To navigate forward to a new screen, you can use the Navigator.push method. For example:

```
Navigator.push(

context,

MaterialPageRoute(builder: (context) => SecondScreen()),

);
```

- To navigate back to the previous screen, you can use the Navigator.pop method:

```
Navigator.pop(context);
```

Named Routes

Named routes provide a more structured way to navigate between screens by assigning unique names to routes. You define named routes in the app's MaterialApp and navigate using these names:

```
MaterialApp(

routes: {

'/second': (context) => SecondScreen(),

},

)
```

To navigate to the named route:

```
Navigator.pushNamed(context, '/second');
```

State Management in Flutter

Managing state is crucial for creating dynamic and responsive apps. Flutter offers several options for managing state, each suited to different scenarios:

Stateful Widgets

Stateful widgets, as mentioned earlier, allow you to maintain mutable state within a widget. This is suitable when a portion of your UI needs to change in response to user interactions.

```
class CounterWidget extends StatefulWidget {

@override

_CounterWidgetState createState() => _CounterWidgetState();
```

```
}
class _CounterWidgetState extends State<CounterWidget> {
int _counter = 0;
void _incrementCounter() {
setState(() {
_counter++;
});
}
@override
Widget build(BuildContext context) {
return Column(
children: [
Text('Counter: $_counter'),
ElevatedButton(
onPressed: _incrementCounter,
child: Text('Increment'),
),
],
);
}
```

```
}
```

Provider

The Provider package is a popular choice for managing state in Flutter apps. It allows you to share data across widgets efficiently.

BLoC (Business Logic Component) Pattern

BLoC is an architectural pattern that separates business logic from the UI. It's an excellent choice for complex apps and offers excellent testability.

```
class CounterBloc {

int _counter = 0;

final _controller = StreamController<int>();

Stream<int> get counterStream => _controller.stream;

void increment() {

_counter++;

_controller.sink.add(_counter);

}

void dispose() {

_controller.close();

}

}
```

These are just a few options for state management in Flutter. Depending on your app's complexity and requirements, you may choose a different approach.

Conclusion

Navigation and state management are fundamental aspects of Flutter app development. By understanding how to navigate between screens and choose the right state management solution, you can create engaging and interactive mobile applications that respond to user interactions and provide a seamless user experience. In the upcoming sections, we'll explore more advanced topics in Flutter development.

Section 12.4: Integrating APIs and Plugins in Flutter

Flutter's power lies not only in its UI capabilities but also in its ability to interact with various APIs and plugins. In this section, we'll delve into the integration of external APIs and plugins within your Flutter applications.

Making API Requests

Many mobile apps require data from external sources, such as web services or databases. Flutter makes it easy to make HTTP requests to retrieve data.

Using the http Package

Flutter provides the http package for making HTTP requests. You can add it to your pubspec.yaml file:

dependencies:

```
http: ^0.13.3
```

Here's an example of making a GET request using the http package:

```
import 'package:http/http.dart' as http;

Future<void> fetchData() async {

final response = await http.get(Uri.parse('https://api.example.com/data'));

if (response.statusCode == 200) {

// Data successfully fetched, parse it here

} else {

// Handle errors

}

}
```

Parsing JSON

When working with REST APIs, the data is often returned in JSON format. You can use Dart's built-in dart:convert library to parse JSON data:

```
import 'dart:convert';

void parseJson(String jsonString) {

final parsedData = json.decode(jsonString);

// Now, you can work with the parsed data

}
```

Using Flutter Plugins

Flutter plugins provide pre-built integrations with native device features or third-party services. You can find a wide range of plugins in the Flutter ecosystem[2].

Adding a Plugin

To use a plugin, add it to your pubspec.yaml file and run flutter pub get. For example, to add the camera plugin:

```
dependencies:

camera: ^0.10.2
```

Accessing Device Features

Plugins like camera allow you to access device-specific features. Here's an example of capturing a photo using the camera plugin:

```
import 'package:camera/camera.dart';

Future<void> takePicture() async {

final cameras = await availableCameras();

final firstCamera = cameras.first;

final controller = CameraController(firstCamera, ResolutionPreset.medium);

await controller.initialize();

final XFile image = await controller.takePicture();
```

2. https://pub.dev/

```
// Handle the captured image
}
```

Conclusion

Integrating APIs and plugins is a crucial aspect of mobile app development. Flutter's flexibility and extensive package ecosystem make it relatively simple to connect your app to external data sources, device features, and third-party services. Whether you're fetching data from a RESTful API or accessing the device's camera, Flutter provides the tools you need to create feature-rich and connected applications. In the next section, we'll explore deploying Flutter apps on both iOS and Android platforms.

Section 12.5: Deploying Flutter Apps on iOS and Android

Once you've developed a Flutter mobile app, the next step is deploying it to actual devices or app stores. This section covers the deployment process for both iOS and Android platforms.

Preparing for Deployment

Before deploying your Flutter app, there are several essential preparations:

1. **Code Review and Testing**: Ensure that your app has been thoroughly tested and reviewed. Address any bugs, performance issues, or user experience problems.
2. **App Icon and Assets**: Set an app icon and ensure that all necessary assets (images, fonts, etc.) are included in your project.
3. **App Configuration**: Configure your app's metadata, such

as its name, version, and description, in the pubspec.yaml file.

Deploying to Android

Building the APK (Android Package)

To deploy your Flutter app on Android, you need to create an APK file. You can do this using the following command:

```
flutter build apk
```

This command generates an APK file in the build/app/outputs/flutter-apk directory of your project. You can then distribute this APK directly to users or upload it to the Google Play Store.

Preparing for Google Play Store

If you plan to publish your app on the Google Play Store, you need to create a developer account, pay a one-time registration fee, and follow Google's guidelines for app submissions.

1. **Create a Developer Account**: Go to the Google Play Console[3], sign in with your Google account, and pay the registration fee.
2. **App Release**: Prepare your app for release by providing details, uploading screenshots, and creating a listing.
3. **App Signing**: Google Play offers the option to use Google's App Signing service, which helps manage the signing keys. Alternatively, you can sign your app using your own key.
4. **Upload APK**: Upload your generated APK to the Google

3. https://play.google.com/console/

Play Console.

5. **Store Listing**: Create a store listing for your app, including descriptions, screenshots, and other promotional materials.
6. **Pricing and Distribution**: Choose pricing options and specify where your app should be available.
7. **Publish**: After completing all the necessary steps, you can publish your app to the Google Play Store.

Deploying to iOS

Building the iOS App

To deploy your Flutter app on iOS, you need to build an iOS binary. This process involves generating an Xcode project and configuring it for deployment.

1. **Generate Xcode Project**: Use the following command to generate an Xcode project:

```
flutter create .
```

1. **Open in Xcode**: Open the generated Xcode project (located in the ios directory) in Xcode.
2. **Configure Signing**: Set up code signing for your app in Xcode. This involves selecting a development team and provisioning profile.
3. **Build for iOS**: Build your Flutter app for iOS using Xcode. You can choose either the simulator or a physical iOS device.

App Store Connect and App Review

Before you can publish your app to the Apple App Store, follow these steps:

1. **Create App Store Connect Account**: Go to App Store Connect[4] and sign in with your Apple ID. Create a new app entry for your app.
2. **App Review**: Prepare your app for Apple's review process. Ensure that it complies with Apple's guidelines and that you provide all required information, screenshots, and app descriptions.
3. **App Store Release**: After passing Apple's review, you can release your app to the App Store.

Conclusion

Deploying a Flutter app to iOS and Android platforms involves several steps, from building the app binaries to preparing app listings and following platform-specific guidelines. Once deployed, your app becomes accessible to a wide audience, and you can manage updates and user engagement through the respective app store portals. This marks the final step in the journey of developing and sharing your Flutter mobile application. In the next and final chapter, we'll explore the future of C# and Flutter development and discuss ways to continue your learning and contribute to the developer community.

4. https://appstoreconnect.apple.com/

Chapter 13: Working with Databases in C

Section 13.1: Introduction to Database Systems

In modern software development, databases play a pivotal role in managing, storing, and retrieving data. Whether you're building a simple application or a complex enterprise-level system, understanding database systems is essential. This section introduces you to the fundamentals of databases and their importance in C# application development.

What Is a Database?

A database is a structured collection of data organized for efficient storage, retrieval, and management. It acts as a centralized repository where data can be stored, updated, and queried. Databases are used to store various types of information, such as user profiles, product catalogs, transaction records, and more.

Types of Databases

There are several types of databases, each designed for specific use cases. The two main categories of databases are:

1. **Relational Databases**: Relational databases store data in tables with predefined schemas. These databases use structured query language (SQL) for data manipulation. Examples include MySQL, PostgreSQL, and Microsoft SQL Server.
2. **NoSQL Databases**: NoSQL databases are schema-less and are suitable for unstructured or semi-structured data. They

provide flexibility and can handle large volumes of data. Examples include MongoDB, Cassandra, and Redis.

Database Management Systems (DBMS)

A Database Management System (DBMS) is software that enables users to interact with databases. It provides tools for creating, querying, updating, and managing databases. Common DBMS types include:

- **SQL DBMS**: These systems, such as MySQL and PostgreSQL, use SQL for data manipulation. They are known for their relational data model.

- **NoSQL DBMS**: NoSQL databases, like MongoDB and Cassandra, are designed for handling unstructured or semi-structured data.

- **In-Memory DBMS**: These databases, such as Redis, store data in memory for ultra-fast access.

- **Columnar DBMS**: Columnar databases like Apache Cassandra are optimized for analytical queries on large datasets.

Data Modeling

Data modeling is the process of defining the structure of the data to be stored in a database. In relational databases, this involves designing tables, defining relationships between tables, and specifying constraints. NoSQL databases often use document-based or key-value data models.

Persistence

Persistence refers to the ability of a database to retain data even after the application that created or modified the data has terminated. Persistence ensures that data remains available across system restarts and failures.

Database Interactions in C

In C# application development, you interact with databases using Database APIs or Object-Relational Mapping (ORM) libraries. Popular choices for working with databases in C# include Entity Framework (EF) for relational databases and libraries like MongoDB.Driver for NoSQL databases.

Understanding database systems and how to interact with them is crucial for building robust and data-driven C# applications. In the following sections of this chapter, we will delve deeper into various aspects of working with databases in C#.

Section 13.2: Connecting to Databases

To work with databases in C#, you need to establish a connection to the database system of your choice. This section covers the fundamental steps for connecting to databases from your C# applications.

Database Connection Strings

In C#, database connections are typically established using connection strings. A connection string is a string that contains the information required to connect to a database, including details like the server's location, credentials, and the database's name. Here's an example of a SQL Server connection string:

```
string connectionString = "Server=localhost;Database=MyDatabase;User Id=myUsername;Password=myPassword;";
```

The exact format of connection strings varies depending on the database system you're using, so be sure to refer to the documentation of your chosen database for the correct syntax.

Using ADO.NET for Database Connections

ADO.NET (ActiveX Data Objects for .NET) is a set of libraries in the .NET Framework that provides data access to various database systems. It allows you to connect to a database, execute SQL commands, and retrieve or manipulate data. Here's a basic example of connecting to a SQL Server database using ADO.NET:

```
using System;

using System.Data.SqlClient;

class Program

{

static void Main()

{

string connectionString = "Server=localhost;Database=MyDatabase;User Id=myUsername;Password=myPassword;";

using (SqlConnection connection = new SqlConnection(connectionString))

{
```

```
try
{
connection.Open();
Console.WriteLine("Connected to the database.");
// Perform database operations here
}
catch (Exception ex)
{
Console.WriteLine($"Error: {ex.Message}");
}
}
}
}
```

In this example, we create a SqlConnection object and open a connection to the SQL Server database using the connection string. Make sure to replace the connection string values with your database credentials.

Connection Pooling

Connection pooling is a technique used to efficiently manage database connections. When a connection is closed, it is not immediately terminated but rather returned to a pool of available connections. This allows for faster connection reuse and reduces the overhead of opening and closing connections for each database operation.

Most ADO.NET database providers, including SqlConnection for SQL Server, automatically enable connection pooling by default. Therefore, you don't need to manage connection pooling explicitly in your code.

Error Handling

When working with database connections, it's important to handle exceptions properly. In the code example above, we used a try-catch block to catch and handle any exceptions that might occur during the database connection process. Proper error handling ensures that your application gracefully handles database-related issues.

Asynchronous Database Operations

In modern C# development, asynchronous programming is common for performing database operations. You can use the async and await keywords to perform database queries asynchronously, which can improve the responsiveness of your applications, especially in scenarios with high database latency.

Connecting to databases is the first step in building data-driven C# applications. Once you've established a connection, you can perform various database operations, including querying, inserting, updating, and deleting data. In the next sections, we'll explore more database-related topics, including SQL database operations and working with Entity Framework for ORM-based database access.

Section 13.3: SQL Database Operations

Once you've established a connection to a database in C#, you'll likely want to perform various database operations such as querying, inserting, updating, and deleting data. In this section, we'll explore the basics of SQL database operations using ADO.NET, which provides a powerful way to work with databases.

Executing SQL Queries

To execute SQL queries against a database, you'll need to use the SqlCommand class in conjunction with your database connection. Here's an example of querying data from a SQL Server database:

```
using System;

using System.Data;

using System.Data.SqlClient;

class Program

{

static void Main()

{

string connectionString = "Server=localhost;Database=MyDatabase;User Id=myUsername;Password=myPassword;";

using (SqlConnection connection = new SqlConnection(connectionString))

{
```

```
try
{
connection.Open();
Console.WriteLine("Connected to the database.");
// SQL query
string sqlQuery = "SELECT Id, Name FROM Customers";
using (SqlCommand command = new SqlCommand(sqlQuery,
connection))
{
using (SqlDataReader reader = command.ExecuteReader())
{
while (reader.Read())
{
int id = reader.GetInt32(0); // Assuming Id is the first column
string name = reader.GetString(1); // Assuming Name is the second
column
Console.WriteLine($"Customer ID: {id}, Name: {name}");
}
}
}
}
```

```
catch (Exception ex)

{

Console.WriteLine($"Error: {ex.Message}");

}

}

}

}
```

In this example, we execute a SELECT query against a Customers table, retrieve the results using a SqlDataReader, and process the data. Make sure to replace the SQL query with your own query as needed.

Executing Non-Query SQL Commands

Apart from querying data, you may need to execute non-query SQL commands like INSERT, UPDATE, or DELETE to modify the database. Here's an example of inserting data into a SQL Server database:

```
using System;

using System.Data;

using System.Data.SqlClient;

class Program

{

static void Main()
```

```
{
string connectionString = "Server=localhost;Database=MyDatabase;User Id=myUsername;Password=myPassword;";
using (SqlConnection connection = new SqlConnection(connectionString))
{
try
{
connection.Open();
Console.WriteLine("Connected to the database.");
// SQL INSERT command
string insertSql = "INSERT INTO Employees (FirstName, LastName) VALUES ('John', 'Doe')";
using (SqlCommand insertCommand = new SqlCommand(insertSql, connection))
{
int rowsAffected = insertCommand.ExecuteNonQuery();
Console.WriteLine($"Rows affected: {rowsAffected}");
}
}
catch (Exception ex)
```

```
{
Console.WriteLine($"Error: {ex.Message}");
}
}
}
}
```

In this example, we execute an INSERT query to add a new employee to an Employees table. The ExecuteNonQuery method is used to execute non-query SQL commands, and it returns the number of rows affected.

Parameterized Queries

When working with SQL queries that involve user input, it's crucial to use parameterized queries to prevent SQL injection attacks. Parameterized queries ensure that user input is treated as data, not as executable SQL code. Here's an example of a parameterized query:

```
using System;
using System.Data;
using System.Data.SqlClient;
class Program
{
static void Main()
{
```

```
string connectionString =
"Server=localhost;Database=MyDatabase;User
Id=myUsername;Password=myPassword;";

using (SqlConnection connection = new
SqlConnection(connectionString))

{

try

{

connection.Open();

Console.WriteLine("Connected to the database.");

// Parameterized SQL query

string sqlQuery = "SELECT Id, Name FROM Products WHERE
Category = @Category";

using (SqlCommand command = new SqlCommand(sqlQuery,
connection))

{

// Define and set the parameter

command.Parameters.Add(new SqlParameter("@Category",
"Electronics"));

using (SqlDataReader reader = command.ExecuteReader())

{

while (reader.Read())
```

```
{
int id = reader.GetInt32(0);
string name = reader.GetString(1);
Console.WriteLine($"Product ID: {id}, Name: {name}");
}
}
}
}
catch (Exception ex)
{
Console.WriteLine($"Error: {ex.Message}");
}
}
}
}
```

In this example, the @Category parameter is used in the SQL query, and we set its value using command.Parameters.Add.

Transactions

Transactions allow you to group a series of SQL operations into a single, atomic unit. Either all the operations within a transaction are executed, or none of them are. This ensures data consistency.

To use transactions with ADO.NET, you can wrap your code in a SqlTransaction:

```
using System;

using System.Data;

using System.Data.SqlClient;

class Program

{

static void Main()
```

##

Section 13.4: Entity Framework and ORM

Entity Framework (EF) **is** an Object-Relational Mapping (ORM) framework that simplifies database access **in** C# applications by allowing you to work with databases **using** object-oriented techniques. It abstracts the low-level database operations and enables you to interact with databases **using** C# classes and LINQ queries. In **this** section, we'll explore the basics of Entity Framework.

Installing Entity Framework

Before you can start **using** Entity Framework, you need to install the Entity Framework package. You can **do this using** NuGet Package Manager **in** Visual Studio or by running the following command **in** the NuGet CLI:

```shell
Install-Package EntityFramework
```

Creating an Entity Data Model

Entity Framework uses an Entity Data Model (EDM) to map database tables to C# classes. You can create an EDM using the Entity Data Model Wizard in Visual Studio. Here are the basic steps to create an EDM:

1. Right-click your project in Solution Explorer.
2. Select "Add" > "New Item..."
3. Choose "Data" from the left menu, then select "ADO.NET Entity Data Model."
4. Follow the wizard to connect to your database and generate the model.

Working with Entity Framework

Once you have created an EDM, you can work with it in your C# code. Here's a simple example of querying data using Entity Framework:

```
using System;

using System.Linq;

class Program

{

static void Main()

{

using (var context = new YourDbContext())

{
```

```
var customers = context.Customers.Where(c => c.City == "New York").ToList();

foreach (var customer in customers)

{

Console.WriteLine($"Customer ID: {customer.CustomerId}, Name: {customer.Name}");

}

}

}

}
```

In this example, we assume you have a Customer entity in your EDM with properties like CustomerId and Name. We use LINQ queries to filter customers in the “New York” city.

Inserting Data

To insert data into the database using Entity Framework, you can create a new entity object, add it to the context, and then call SaveChanges:

```
using System;

class Program

{

static void Main()

{
```

```
using (var context = new YourDbContext())

{

var newCustomer = new Customer { Name = "John Doe", City =
"Los Angeles" };

context.Customers.Add(newCustomer);

context.SaveChanges();

}

}

}
```

In this example, we create a new Customer object, add it to the context, and then call SaveChanges to persist it in the database.

Updating and Deleting Data

Updating and deleting data with Entity Framework is straightforward. You can retrieve an entity, modify its properties, and then call SaveChanges:

```
using System;

using System.Linq;

class Program

{

static void Main()

{

using (var context = new YourDbContext())
```

```
{
var customer = context.Customers.FirstOrDefault(c =>
c.CustomerId == 1);
if (customer != null)
{
customer.City = "Chicago"; // Update the city
context.SaveChanges();
}
}
}
}
```

To delete an entity, you can remove it from the context and then call SaveChanges:

```
using System;
using System.Linq;
class Program
{
static void Main()
{
using (var context = new YourDbContext())
{
```

```
var customer = context.Customers.FirstOrDefault(c => c.CustomerId == 1);

if (customer != null)

{

context.Customers.Remove(customer); // Delete the customer

context.SaveChanges();

}

}

}

}
```

Summary

Entity Framework simplifies database access by providing an object-oriented approach to interact with databases. It's a powerful tool for C# developers, allowing you to work with databases using C# classes and LINQ queries while abstracting away the complexities of database operations. Whether you're querying data, inserting, updating, or deleting records, Entity Framework can streamline your database-related tasks and improve code maintainability.

Section 13.5: NoSQL and Document Databases

In this section, we'll explore NoSQL databases and their use in C# applications. NoSQL databases are a type of database management system that provides a flexible and schema-less way of storing and retrieving data. Unlike traditional relational databases, which use structured tables, NoSQL databases store data in various formats such as JSON, BSON, XML, or key-value pairs. One popular category of NoSQL databases is document databases.

Document Databases

Document databases, as the name suggests, store data in documents. These documents can be in formats like JSON or BSON and are typically hierarchical, allowing for nested data structures. MongoDB is a well-known document database that is often used with C# applications.

Installing the MongoDB C# Driver

To work with MongoDB in C#, you need to install the MongoDB C# driver. You can do this using NuGet Package Manager with the following command:

```
Install-Package MongoDB.Driver
```

Connecting to MongoDB

Here's a basic example of connecting to a MongoDB database from a C# application:

```
using MongoDB.Driver;

class Program

{

static void Main()

{
```

```
// Replace 'your_connection_string' with your MongoDB connection string
var client = new MongoClient("your_connection_string");
// Access a specific database
var database = client.GetDatabase("your_database_name");
// Access a collection within the database
var collection = database.GetCollection<BsonDocument>("your_collection_name");
// Now you can work with the collection
// ...
}
}
```

CRUD Operations with MongoDB

MongoDB supports the basic CRUD (Create, Read, Update, Delete) operations. Here's a brief overview of how to perform these operations in C#:

- **Inserting Documents:**

```
var document = new BsonDocument
{
{ "name", "John Doe" },
{ "age", 30 }
```

```
};
collection.InsertOne(document);
```

- **Querying Documents:**

```
var filter = Builders<BsonDocument>.Filter.Eq("name", "John Doe");
var result = collection.Find(filter).ToList();
```

- **Updating Documents:**

```
var filter = Builders<BsonDocument>.Filter.Eq("name", "John Doe");
var update = Builders<BsonDocument>.Update.Set("age", 31);
collection.UpdateOne(filter, update);
```

- **Deleting Documents:**

```
var filter = Builders<BsonDocument>.Filter.Eq("name", "John Doe");
collection.DeleteOne(filter);
```

Pros and Cons of NoSQL Document Databases

Document databases like MongoDB offer several advantages, such as flexibility, scalability, and support for nested data structures. They are a good choice for applications that need to store unstructured or semi-structured data.

However, document databases may not be suitable for all scenarios. They lack support for complex joins and transactions, which are common in relational databases. Therefore, the choice between a document database and a relational database depends on your application's specific requirements.

In summary, NoSQL document databases are a valuable addition to the C# developer's toolkit, providing a flexible and scalable way to store and query data. However, it's essential to evaluate your project's needs and requirements carefully before choosing a database type.

Chapter 14: Building Web Applications with ASP.NET Core

Section 14.1: Creating ASP.NET Core Web Applications

ASP.NET Core is a popular open-source web framework developed by Microsoft for building modern web applications. It's a cross-platform framework that allows you to build web applications that can run on Windows, Linux, and macOS. In this section, we'll explore how to create ASP.NET Core web applications using C#.

Prerequisites

Before we get started, make sure you have the following prerequisites installed:

1. **Visual Studio**: You can download and install Visual Studio from the official Microsoft website.
2. **.NET SDK**: Install the .NET SDK, which includes the tools and libraries needed for ASP.NET Core development. You can download it from the .NET website.

Creating a New ASP.NET Core Project

Let's start by creating a new ASP.NET Core project. Follow these steps:

1. Open Visual Studio.
2. Click on "File" -> "New" -> "Project..."
3. In the "Create a new project" dialog, search for "ASP.NET Core Web Application" and select it.
4. Click "Next."

5. Choose a project name, location, and solution name, then click "Create."
6. In the "Create a new ASP.NET Core web application" dialog, select the template that suits your project. You can choose from templates like "Web Application," "API," "MVC," and more. For this example, we'll choose the "Web Application" template.
7. Configure additional settings such as authentication and Docker support if needed.
8. Click "Create."

Understanding the Project Structure

An ASP.NET Core web application consists of several folders and files. Here's a brief overview of the most important ones:

• **wwwroot**: This folder contains static files such as CSS, JavaScript, and images that are served directly to clients.

• **Controllers**: Controllers handle HTTP requests and define the application's behavior.

• **Views**: Views contain the HTML templates that are rendered to produce the user interface.

• **Startup.cs**: This file contains the configuration and middleware setup for your application.

• **appsettings.json**: Configuration settings for the application.

Creating a Basic Web Page

Let's create a basic web page and controller to display "Hello, ASP.NET Core!" on the homepage.

1. In the "Controllers" folder, create a new controller class named HomeController.cs. Add the following code:

```
using Microsoft.AspNetCore.Mvc;

public class HomeController : Controller

{

public IActionResult Index()

{

return View();

}

}
```

1. In the "Views" folder, create a new folder named "Home" and inside it, create a new view file named Index.cshtml. Add the following HTML code:

```
<!DOCTYPE html>

<html>

<head>

<title>My ASP.NET Core App</title>

</head>
```

<body>

<h1>Hello, ASP.NET Core!**</h1>**

</body>

</html>

1. Build and run your application. You should see "Hello, ASP.NET Core!" displayed in your web browser.

Congratulations! You've created a basic ASP.NET Core web application. In the following sections, we'll dive deeper into ASP.NET Core's features and explore how to build more complex web applications.

Section 14.2: Routing and Middleware in ASP.NET Core

In ASP.NET Core, routing and middleware play a crucial role in handling HTTP requests and shaping the behavior of your web application. In this section, we'll explore routing and middleware concepts in ASP.NET Core.

Routing in ASP.NET Core

Routing is the process of determining which controller and action method should handle an incoming HTTP request. ASP.NET Core provides a powerful routing system that allows you to define URL patterns and map them to specific controllers and actions.

Here's how routing works in ASP.NET Core:

1. **Route Templates**: Route templates are defined in controllers using attributes. These templates specify the

URL pattern that triggers a particular action method. For example, [Route("products/{id}")] would match URLs like /products/123.

2. **Route Constraints**: You can apply constraints to route parameters to restrict the values they can accept. For instance, you can specify that the id parameter must be an integer.
3. **Route Parameters**: Route parameters are placeholders in route templates that capture values from the URL. These values are passed as arguments to the action method.
4. **Route Names**: Routes can be named, allowing you to generate URLs based on route names instead of hardcoding URLs.

Here's an example of defining a route in a controller:

```
[Route("products/{id:int}")]

public IActionResult ProductDetails(int id)

{

// Handle the request and display product details.

}
```

Middleware in ASP.NET Core

Middleware components are software components that participate in processing an HTTP request. They can perform various tasks such as authentication, logging, compression, and more. Middleware components are executed in the order they are added to the pipeline.

The ASP.NET Core request processing pipeline consists of multiple middleware components that execute sequentially. Here's a simplified view of the pipeline:

1. **HTTP Request**: An HTTP request enters the pipeline.
2. **Middleware**: Middleware components in the pipeline can perform tasks such as routing, authentication, and authorization.
3. **Controller Action**: Once routing middleware determines the controller and action method to invoke, the action method is executed.
4. **Middleware (Again)**: After the action method execution, additional middleware components can perform post-processing tasks.
5. **HTTP Response**: The HTTP response is generated and sent back to the client.

You can add middleware components to the pipeline in the Startup.cs file. For example, to add authentication middleware, you can use:

```
public void Configure(IApplicationBuilder app, IWebHostEnvironment env)

{

// Other middleware components

app.UseAuthentication(); // Add authentication middleware

// More middleware components

}
```

Middleware components are a fundamental part of ASP.NET Core, and you can even create custom middleware to suit your application's specific needs.

Putting It All Together

Routing and middleware work together to handle HTTP requests in ASP.NET Core. The routing system determines which controller and action method should handle a request based on the URL, and middleware components can perform various tasks before and after controller action execution.

Understanding routing and middleware is essential for building robust and flexible web applications in ASP.NET Core. In subsequent sections, we'll explore more advanced topics and techniques for building web applications with this powerful framework.

Section 14.3: Razor Pages and MVC

In ASP.NET Core, Razor Pages and the Model-View-Controller (MVC) pattern are two fundamental approaches to building web applications. In this section, we'll delve into these approaches and explore when to use each one.

Razor Pages

Razor Pages is a web application framework that focuses on simplicity and productivity. It's an ideal choice for building small to medium-sized applications where a simple and straightforward structure is sufficient.

Key characteristics of Razor Pages:

1. **Page-Oriented**: Razor Pages are organized around individual web pages, each represented by a .cshtml file. Each Razor Page can contain both the view (HTML markup) and the code-behind (C# code).
2. **Convention over Configuration**: Razor Pages follow a convention-based approach. By default, a Razor Page named Index.cshtml in a folder corresponds to the root URL of that folder. This convention simplifies routing.
3. **Model Binding**: Razor Pages have built-in support for model binding, making it easy to work with form data and URL parameters. Page models are responsible for handling user input and responding to requests.
4. **Partial Pages**: Reusable page sections called "partial pages" can be created and included in multiple Razor Pages, promoting code reusability.

Here's a basic example of a Razor Page:

```
<!—Pages/Index.cshtml—>

@page

@model IndexModel

<h1>Welcome to My Website</h1>

<p>Hello, @Model.UserName!</p>

// Pages/Index.cshtml.cs (code-behind)

public class IndexModel : PageModel

{

public string UserName { get; set; }
```

```
public void OnGet()
{
UserName = "John";
}
}
```

Model-View-Controller (MVC)

MVC is a widely adopted architectural pattern for building web applications. It provides a more structured approach suitable for large and complex applications.

Key components of MVC:

1. **Model**: Represents the application's data and business logic. Models are responsible for retrieving and storing data.
2. **View**: Represents the presentation layer and is responsible for rendering the user interface. Views receive data from the model and display it to users.
3. **Controller**: Acts as an intermediary between the model and view. Controllers handle incoming requests, interact with models to retrieve data, and pass that data to views for rendering.

MVC offers a separation of concerns, making it easier to maintain and scale applications. It's a great choice when you need precise control over routing and a more modular code structure.

Here's a simplified example of MVC:

```
// Controller
```

```
public class HomeController : Controller
{
public IActionResult Index()
{
var userName = "Jane";
return View("Index", userName);
}
}
<!—Views/Home/Index.cshtml—>
@model string
<h1>Welcome to My Website</h1>
<p>Hello, @Model!</p>
```

Choosing Between Razor Pages and MVC

The choice between Razor Pages and MVC depends on your application's complexity and requirements. Here are some guidelines:

- Use **Razor Pages** for small to medium-sized applications, prototypes, or scenarios where simplicity and rapid development are essential.
- Choose **MVC** for larger applications with more complex requirements, where a clear separation of

concerns, flexibility in routing, and fine-grained control over components is needed.

Both Razor Pages and MVC are first-class citizens in ASP.NET Core, and you can even combine them in a single application if it suits your needs. Ultimately, the choice should align with your project's specific goals and constraints.

Section 14.4: Authentication and Authorization

Authentication and authorization are critical aspects of web application security. In this section, we'll explore these two concepts and how they are implemented in ASP.NET Core.

Authentication

Authentication is the process of verifying the identity of a user or system. It answers the question, "Who are you?" Users are typically required to provide credentials (such as a username and password) to prove their identity. ASP.NET Core provides robust authentication mechanisms, including:

1. **Cookie-based Authentication**: This method uses encrypted cookies to track authenticated users. Once a user logs in, a cookie is issued, and subsequent requests include this cookie to authenticate the user.
2. **Token-based Authentication**: Token-based authentication, often used for web APIs, involves the issuance of a JSON Web Token (JWT) upon successful login. The token is then included in the request headers for subsequent authentication.
3. **External Authentication**: ASP.NET Core supports

external authentication providers like Google, Facebook, and Microsoft. Users can log in using their existing accounts on these platforms.

Here's a simplified example of setting up cookie-based authentication in an ASP.NET Core application:

```
// Startup.cs
public void ConfigureServices(IServiceCollection services)
{
// ...
services.AddAuthentication(CookieAuthenticationDefaults.Authenticatic
.AddCookie(options =>
{
options.LoginPath = "/Account/Login";
options.AccessDeniedPath = "/Account/AccessDenied";
});
// ...
}
// AccountController.cs
[AllowAnonymous]
public IActionResult Login()
{
```

```
// Your login logic here
return View();
}
[HttpPost]
[AllowAnonymous]
public async Task<IActionResult> Login(LoginViewModel model)
{
// Authenticate the user
// ...
return RedirectToAction("Index", "Home");
}
```

Authorization

Authorization, on the other hand, determines what authenticated users are allowed to do within the application. It answers the question, "What are you allowed to do?" ASP.NET Core offers flexible authorization mechanisms, such as:

1. **Role-based Authorization**: Users are assigned roles, and permissions are associated with these roles. Controllers or actions can be decorated with [Authorize(Roles = "Admin")] to restrict access to users with specific roles.
2. **Policy-based Authorization**: More fine-grained control is achieved by defining policies. Policies can be used to specify complex access requirements based on roles, claims, or custom criteria.

Here's a simple example of role-based authorization:

```
// MyController.cs
[Authorize(Roles = "Admin")]
public class AdminController : Controller
{
// Actions only accessible to users in the "Admin" role
// ...
}
```

Combining Authentication and Authorization

Authentication and authorization often go hand in hand. Once a user is authenticated, authorization rules determine which parts of the application they can access. ASP.NET Core's flexible and customizable middleware allows you to easily integrate these processes into your web application, ensuring that users' identities are verified and their access is controlled appropriately.

In summary, authentication verifies a user's identity, while authorization defines what actions or resources they can access. Implementing these security measures is crucial for protecting your ASP.NET Core web application and its data.

Section 14.5: Real-time Web Applications with SignalR

In modern web applications, real-time communication between clients and the server is becoming increasingly important. Users expect features like instant messaging, live updates, and interactive collaboration. ASP.NET Core provides SignalR, a library that simplifies the implementation of real-time functionality in web applications.

What is SignalR?

SignalR is an open-source library for ASP.NET Core that enables real-time, bidirectional communication between clients and the server. It abstracts the underlying transport mechanisms (WebSockets, Server-Sent Events, Long Polling, etc.) to provide a consistent API for building real-time web applications.

Key Features of SignalR:

1. **Real-time Communication**: SignalR allows server-to-client and client-to-server communication in real time. This is ideal for applications like chat rooms, live notifications, and collaborative tools.
2. **Cross-Platform Support**: SignalR works across various platforms, including web browsers, mobile devices, and desktop applications, making it versatile for building cross-platform solutions.
3. **Multiple Transport Protocols**: It supports multiple transport protocols, falling back to the most suitable one for the client's capabilities. This ensures that real-time features work even in environments with limited support for WebSockets.
4. **Hub-based Model**: SignalR uses a hub-based model, where the server and clients communicate through hubs. Hubs are like channels or groups where messages can be sent and received.
5. **Authentication and Authorization**: SignalR seamlessly integrates with ASP.NET Core's authentication and

authorization systems, allowing you to control access to real-time features.

Getting Started with SignalR

To get started with SignalR in an ASP.NET Core application, you'll need to follow these basic steps:

1. **Install the SignalR Package**: Add the SignalR package to your project using NuGet Package Manager.
2. **Create a Hub**: Create a SignalR hub that defines the methods clients can call and the events they can listen to.
3. **Configure SignalR**: In your Startup.cs file, configure SignalR by adding it to the middleware pipeline.
4. **Client-Side Code**: Implement the SignalR client in your web application's JavaScript or TypeScript code.

Here's a simplified example of setting up a SignalR hub and client:

Server-Side Code (Hub):

```
using Microsoft.AspNetCore.SignalR;

public class ChatHub : Hub

{

public async Task SendMessage(string user, string message)

{

await Clients.All.SendAsync("ReceiveMessage", user, message);

}

}
```

Client-Side Code (JavaScript):

```
const connection = new signalR.HubConnectionBuilder()
.withUrl("/chatHub")
.build();
connection.on("ReceiveMessage", (user, message) => {
// Handle received message
});
connection.start().then(() => {
// Connection established
}).catch(err => {
console.error(err);
});
// Sending a message
connection.invoke("SendMessage", user, message);
```

Use Cases for SignalR

SignalR is versatile and can be used for various real-time scenarios:

- **Chat Applications**: Building chat rooms and instant messaging features.
- **Live Notifications**: Notifying users about updates or events in real time.

- **Collaborative Tools**: Enabling real-time collaboration in applications like document editors or whiteboards.

- **Online Gaming**: Implementing real-time game interactions and multiplayer features.

- **Monitoring Dashboards**: Creating dashboards that update in real time with live data.

- **IoT Control**: Controlling and monitoring IoT devices in real time.

SignalR simplifies the development of these features, making it a valuable addition to your ASP.NET Core toolbox for building interactive and engaging web applications.

Chapter 15: Advanced Web Development Topics

Section 15.1: Dependency Injection in ASP.NET Core

Dependency injection is a fundamental concept in modern software development, and ASP.NET Core makes it easy to implement. Dependency injection allows you to manage the dependencies of your application in a clean and maintainable way. In this section, we'll explore what dependency injection is and how it can be leveraged in ASP.NET Core.

What Is Dependency Injection?

Dependency injection is a design pattern that helps you achieve loose coupling between the components of your application. It allows you to provide the required dependencies (objects or services) to a class rather than having the class create them itself. This promotes code reusability, testability, and maintainability.

In ASP.NET Core, dependency injection is built into the framework. It provides a way to register and resolve services throughout your application. Services can be anything from database connections, configuration settings, or custom application-specific components.

Setting Up Dependency Injection

To use dependency injection in ASP.NET Core, you start by registering your services in the built-in dependency injection container during application startup. This is typically done in the

Startup.cs file within the ConfigureServices method. Here's an example of how you can register a service:

```
public void ConfigureServices(IServiceCollection services)
{
services.AddScoped<IMyService, MyService>();
}
```

In this example, IMyService is an interface representing the service, and MyService is the concrete implementation. The AddScoped method specifies that a new instance of MyService should be created for each HTTP request.

Injecting Dependencies into Controllers

Once services are registered, you can inject them into your controllers or other components that need them. ASP.NET Core's built-in dependency injection container will automatically provide the required services when a controller is created.

```
public class MyController : Controller
{
private readonly IMyService _myService;
public MyController(IMyService myService)
{
_myService = myService;
}
}
```

In this example, IMyService is injected into the MyController constructor. ASP.NET Core will resolve and provide the appropriate implementation of IMyService when a request is made to the MyController action.

Benefits of Dependency Injection

Dependency injection in ASP.NET Core offers several benefits:

1. **Testability:** By injecting dependencies, you can easily substitute real implementations with mock objects during unit testing, making your code more testable.
2. **Maintainability:** Changes to service implementations can be isolated, reducing the impact on other parts of the application.
3. **Flexibility:** You can switch implementations or configurations without altering the dependent code.
4. **Scalability:** Managing the lifetime of services (e.g., transient, scoped, or singleton) is straightforward, ensuring efficient resource usage.

In summary, dependency injection is a crucial aspect of ASP.NET Core development, enabling you to create more maintainable, testable, and flexible applications. Understanding and utilizing this pattern can significantly enhance the quality of your web applications.

Section 15.2: Building RESTful APIs with ASP.NET Core

Building RESTful APIs (Representational State Transfer) is a common requirement for modern web applications. REST is an architectural style for designing networked applications, and

ASP.NET Core provides excellent support for creating RESTful APIs. In this section, we'll explore the key concepts and steps to build RESTful APIs using ASP.NET Core.

What Is a RESTful API?

A RESTful API is an application programming interface that follows the principles of REST. These principles include using standard HTTP methods (GET, POST, PUT, DELETE) for performing operations on resources, representing resources as URIs, and using standard HTTP status codes to indicate the result of API requests.

RESTful APIs are known for their simplicity, scalability, and statelessness. They are widely used for client-server communication in web and mobile applications.

Creating an ASP.NET Core Web API

To create a RESTful API with ASP.NET Core, you can start with an empty ASP.NET Core project or use a template like the "ASP.NET Core Web API" template provided by Visual Studio or the .NET CLI.

Here are the high-level steps to create an ASP.NET Core Web API:

1. **Create a New Project:** Use your preferred development environment to create a new ASP.NET Core Web API project.
2. **Define Data Models:** Define the data models (entities) that your API will work with. These models represent the resources your API will expose.
3. **Create Controllers:** Create controllers that define the API endpoints and actions. Each action corresponds to a

specific HTTP method (GET, POST, PUT, DELETE) and maps to a resource or operation.

4. **Implement CRUD Operations:** In the controller actions, implement the CRUD (Create, Read, Update, Delete) operations for your resources. Use Entity Framework Core or another data access library to interact with the database.
5. **Route Configuration:** Configure routing in Startup.cs to define how URLs map to controller actions. This can be done using attributes like [Route] or by configuring routes in the Startup class.
6. **Testing:** Test your API using tools like Postman, curl, or client libraries for your programming language of choice.
7. **Authentication and Authorization:** Implement authentication and authorization mechanisms to secure your API endpoints if required.

Example Controller Action for GET Operation

Here's an example of a simple controller action for retrieving a list of items:

```
[HttpGet]

public IActionResult GetItems()

{

var items = _repository.GetItems(); // Fetch items from a data repository

return Ok(items); // Return a 200 OK response with the items

}
```

In this example, the [HttpGet] attribute specifies that this action responds to HTTP GET requests. The GetItems method retrieves items from a data repository and returns them as the response with a 200 OK status.

Testing Your API

To test your API during development, you can use tools like Postman or write unit tests using testing frameworks like xUnit or NUnit. It's essential to validate that your API behaves as expected and handles various scenarios.

Building RESTful APIs with ASP.NET Core allows you to create scalable and interoperable services that can be consumed by a wide range of clients, including web applications, mobile apps, and other services. Understanding REST principles and following best practices for API design are key to developing robust APIs.

Section 15.3: Microservices Architecture

Microservices architecture is a software design pattern that has gained significant popularity in recent years. It is an architectural style where an application is composed of multiple small, independent services that communicate with each other through well-defined APIs. Each service is responsible for a specific set of functionalities, and they can be developed, deployed, and scaled independently. In this section, we'll explore the key concepts of microservices architecture and its advantages.

Key Concepts of Microservices

1. **Decomposition:** In a microservices architecture, a monolithic application is decomposed into a collection of loosely coupled services. Each service focuses on a specific

business capability, such as user management, product catalog, or payment processing.
2. **Independence:** Microservices are independent entities that can be developed, deployed, and maintained separately. This independence allows teams to work on different services concurrently, facilitating faster development and deployment.
3. **Communication:** Microservices communicate with each other through well-defined APIs. This can be achieved using RESTful APIs, message queues, or other communication mechanisms. Loose coupling between services ensures that changes in one service do not adversely affect others.
4. **Scaling:** Services can be scaled independently based on their specific needs. For example, a service experiencing high traffic can be scaled horizontally to handle increased load, while other services remain unchanged.
5. **Technology Diversity:** Microservices enable the use of different technologies and programming languages for each service. Teams can choose the best technology stack for the specific requirements of their service.

Advantages of Microservices Architecture

1. **Scalability:** Microservices allow you to scale individual components of your application based on demand, leading to efficient resource utilization and cost savings.
2. **Faster Development:** Smaller, focused teams can develop and release services independently, speeding up the development process.
3. **Flexibility:** You can choose the most suitable technology stack for each service, allowing you to leverage the strengths of different programming languages and

frameworks.

4. **Fault Isolation:** Issues in one service are less likely to affect the entire application, as failures are isolated to the faulty service.
5. **Easier Maintenance:** Smaller codebases are easier to maintain and debug. Updates and changes can be made with less risk of unintended consequences.

Challenges of Microservices

While microservices offer several advantages, they also introduce challenges:

1. **Complexity:** Managing a large number of services can become complex, requiring robust monitoring, logging, and orchestration tools.
2. **Data Management:** Handling data consistency and sharing among services can be challenging, requiring careful design and synchronization mechanisms.
3. **Deployment and Orchestration:** Coordinating the deployment of multiple services and ensuring they work together seamlessly can be challenging.
4. **Testing:** Testing microservices requires a strategy for unit testing, integration testing, and end-to-end testing.
5. **Security:** Securing a distributed system with multiple services requires careful consideration of authentication, authorization, and data protection.

In conclusion, microservices architecture offers a scalable and flexible approach to building software systems. However, it comes with its own set of challenges that need to be carefully addressed. When implemented correctly, microservices can enable agility, faster development, and better resource utilization in modern software development projects.

Section 15.4: Containerization with Docker

Docker is a powerful tool for containerization, which has revolutionized the way applications are developed, shipped, and run. Containers are lightweight, standalone, and executable packages that contain everything needed to run a piece of software, including the code, runtime, system tools, libraries, and settings. Docker provides a platform for developing, shipping, and running applications within containers. In this section, we'll explore Docker and its significance in modern software development.

Understanding Docker

Docker is based on containerization technology, which allows you to create and run containers on a host system. Containers are isolated from each other and from the host system, making them an ideal choice for packaging applications and their dependencies. Here are some key concepts related to Docker:

1. **Images:** Docker uses images as templates to create containers. An image is a read-only file that contains a snapshot of a software application, including its code, libraries, and configurations.
2. **Containers:** Containers are instances of Docker images. They are lightweight, runnable environments that can execute the software defined in the image. Containers are isolated from one another and from the host system.
3. **Dockerfile:** A Dockerfile is a text file that contains instructions for building a Docker image. It specifies the base image, the application code, and any necessary

configurations.

4. **Docker Hub:** Docker Hub is a cloud-based registry that hosts thousands of Docker images. It allows you to easily share and distribute Docker images.

Benefits of Docker

Docker offers several advantages for software development and deployment:

1. **Consistency:** Docker ensures that applications run consistently across different environments, from development to production. This reduces the "it works on my machine" problem.
2. **Isolation:** Containers provide process and file system isolation, preventing conflicts between different applications and dependencies.
3. **Portability:** Docker containers can run on any system that supports Docker, making it easy to move applications between different infrastructure environments.
4. **Resource Efficiency:** Containers are lightweight and share the host OS kernel, leading to efficient resource utilization and faster startup times.
5. **Scalability:** Docker makes it easy to scale applications horizontally by creating multiple container instances of the same image.

Docker in Practice

To use Docker effectively, you need to follow these steps:

1. **Write a Dockerfile:** Create a Dockerfile that defines the image you want to build. Specify the base image, copy your application code, and configure the environment.

2. **Build the Image:** Use the docker build command to build an image from the Dockerfile. This image can be versioned and shared.
3. **Run Containers:** Create and run containers from the images you've built using the docker run command. You can specify container-specific configurations at runtime.
4. **Orchestration:** For managing multiple containers and scaling applications, consider using orchestration tools like Kubernetes or Docker Compose.

Docker has become a fundamental tool in modern software development and deployment pipelines. It enables developers to package applications with their dependencies, ensuring consistent and reliable execution across different environments. When combined with container orchestration solutions, Docker becomes a powerful tool for building scalable and resilient microservices architectures.

Section 15.5: Deploying Web Applications to the Cloud

Cloud computing has transformed the way applications are developed, deployed, and managed. It offers a scalable and cost-effective solution for hosting web applications, making it possible to reach a global audience without the need for extensive infrastructure management. In this section, we'll explore the process of deploying web applications to the cloud and discuss some popular cloud providers and services.

Benefits of Cloud Deployment

Deploying web applications to the cloud provides several advantages:

1. **Scalability:** Cloud platforms allow you to easily scale your application based on demand. You can add or remove resources as needed, ensuring optimal performance and cost-effectiveness.
2. **Global Reach:** Cloud providers offer data centers in multiple regions worldwide. This enables you to deploy your application closer to your users, reducing latency and improving the user experience.
3. **Cost Efficiency:** Cloud services often follow a pay-as-you-go model, where you only pay for the resources you use. This eliminates the need for large upfront investments in infrastructure.
4. **High Availability:** Cloud providers offer redundancy and failover mechanisms, ensuring that your application remains available even in the event of hardware failures.
5. **Managed Services:** Cloud platforms offer a wide range of managed services, such as databases, caching, and content delivery networks (CDNs), which can simplify development and reduce operational overhead.

Cloud Service Models

When deploying web applications to the cloud, you can choose from different service models:

1. **Infrastructure as a Service (IaaS):** In the IaaS model, you rent virtualized hardware resources, such as virtual machines and storage, from the cloud provider. You have full control over the operating system and software stack but are responsible for managing and maintaining them.
2. **Platform as a Service (PaaS):** PaaS provides a higher-level abstraction, allowing you to focus on application development rather than infrastructure management. The

cloud provider handles the underlying infrastructure, including the operating system and runtime environment.

3. **Serverless Computing:** Serverless computing abstracts away servers completely. You only pay for the execution of code in response to events, and the cloud provider automatically manages the infrastructure. AWS Lambda, Azure Functions, and Google Cloud Functions are examples of serverless platforms.

Popular Cloud Providers

Several cloud providers offer a range of services for deploying web applications:

1. **Amazon Web Services (AWS):** AWS is one of the largest and most popular cloud providers. It offers a vast array of services, including EC2 for virtual machines, S3 for object storage, and AWS Lambda for serverless computing.
2. **Microsoft Azure:** Azure provides a comprehensive suite of cloud services and is known for its integration with Microsoft technologies. Azure App Service is a PaaS offering for web application hosting.
3. **Google Cloud Platform (GCP):** GCP offers a wide range of cloud services, including Google App Engine for PaaS and Google Kubernetes Engine (GKE) for container orchestration.
4. **IBM Cloud:** IBM Cloud provides a variety of cloud services and solutions, with a focus on hybrid and multicloud environments. IBM Cloud Foundry offers a PaaS option for web applications.
5. **Heroku:** Heroku is a cloud platform that simplifies application deployment. It abstracts away infrastructure management, making it easy to deploy web applications

using various programming languages.

Deployment Strategies

When deploying web applications to the cloud, consider the following strategies:

1. **Continuous Integration and Continuous Deployment (CI/CD):** Implement CI/CD pipelines to automate the building, testing, and deployment of your application, ensuring a consistent and efficient release process.
2. **Load Balancing:** Use load balancers to distribute incoming traffic across multiple instances of your application, improving scalability and availability.
3. **Database Scaling:** Depending on your database needs, choose between managed database services or database scaling strategies like sharding and replication.
4. **Content Delivery:** Utilize content delivery networks (CDNs) to cache and distribute static assets, reducing latency and improving load times for users worldwide.
5. **Monitoring and Scaling:** Implement monitoring and alerting solutions to track the performance and health of your application. Use auto-scaling to automatically adjust resources based on demand.

Deploying web applications to the cloud offers flexibility, scalability, and reliability, making it a compelling choice for businesses of all sizes. By leveraging the benefits of cloud computing and choosing the right cloud provider and service model, you can efficiently host and manage web applications that meet the needs of your users and your organization.

Chapter 16: Security in C

Section 16.1: Authentication and Authorization Techniques

Security is a critical aspect of software development, especially in applications that handle sensitive data or interact with users. Authentication and authorization are fundamental techniques for ensuring that only authorized users have access to certain parts of an application or specific functionalities. In this section, we will explore the concepts of authentication and authorization in C# applications and various techniques to implement them securely.

Authentication vs. Authorization

Before diving into the techniques, it's essential to understand the difference between authentication and authorization:

- **Authentication:** Authentication is the process of verifying the identity of a user, device, or system component. It answers the question, "Who are you?" Common authentication methods include username and password, multi-factor authentication (MFA), and token-based authentication.

- **Authorization:** Authorization comes after authentication and determines what actions or resources an authenticated user or entity is allowed to access. It answers the question, "What are you allowed to do?" Authorization is often expressed through roles, permissions, or access control lists (ACLs).

Authentication Techniques

1. **Username and Password:** This is one of the most common authentication methods. Users provide a username and a secret password, which is hashed and compared to the stored hash. Libraries like ASP.NET Identity provide built-in support for this method.
2. **Multi-Factor Authentication (MFA):** MFA adds an extra layer of security by requiring users to provide two or more forms of identification. This could include something they know (password), something they have (a security token), or something they are (biometric data).
3. **Token-Based Authentication:** Token-based authentication involves issuing a token to an authenticated user, which is then included in subsequent requests. JSON Web Tokens (JWTs) are a popular choice for implementing this method.
4. **OAuth and OpenID Connect:** These protocols are widely used for authenticating users via third-party identity providers (e.g., social media accounts). OAuth focuses on authorization, while OpenID Connect adds an authentication layer on top of OAuth.

Authorization Techniques

1. **Role-Based Access Control (RBAC):** RBAC assigns users to roles, and each role is associated with specific permissions. Users inherit permissions based on their assigned roles. ASP.NET Core's Identity system supports RBAC.
2. **Attribute-Based Access Control (ABAC):** ABAC evaluates attributes (e.g., user attributes, resource attributes) to make access control decisions. This dynamic

approach allows fine-grained control.

3. **Claims-Based Authorization:** In this approach, claims (pieces of information about the user) are used to make authorization decisions. Policies are defined based on claims, and these policies determine access.
4. **Resource-Based Authorization:** Resource-based authorization uses the attributes of a resource (e.g., a file, a database record) to determine access. Access control lists (ACLs) and role-based resource control are examples of this technique.

Best Practices for Security

When implementing authentication and authorization in your C# applications, consider these best practices:

- **Always Hash Passwords:** When storing passwords, hash them using strong cryptographic hashing algorithms (e.g., bcrypt, Argon2). Never store plain-text passwords.

- **Implement Proper Session Management:** Ensure that user sessions are managed securely, with session tokens that are hard to guess or steal.

- **Use HTTPS:** Secure your application with HTTPS to encrypt data in transit and protect against man-in-the-middle attacks.

- **Regularly Update Libraries and Frameworks:** Keep your authentication and authorization libraries and frameworks up to date to patch known security vulnerabilities.

- **Implement Rate Limiting and Brute Force Protection:** Protect against brute force attacks by implementing rate limiting and account lockout mechanisms.

- **Security Testing:** Regularly conduct security testing, including penetration testing and code reviews, to identify and mitigate security vulnerabilities.

Authentication and authorization are critical components of securing your C# applications. By understanding the principles and implementing secure techniques, you can protect your application and user data from unauthorized access and potential security threats.

Section 16.2: Securing Web Applications

Securing web applications is of paramount importance to protect both user data and the application itself. In this section, we'll explore various strategies and best practices for securing web applications developed in C#.

1. Input Validation

One of the most common security vulnerabilities in web applications is improper input validation. Always validate user inputs to prevent attacks like SQL injection, cross-site scripting (XSS), and cross-site request forgery (CSRF).

```
// Example of input validation in ASP.NET Core

public IActionResult Search(string query)

{
```

```
if (string.IsNullOrWhiteSpace(query))
{
// Handle invalid input
return BadRequest("Invalid query.");
}
// Process the query
// ...
}
```

2. Cross-Site Scripting (XSS) Prevention

XSS attacks occur when an attacker injects malicious scripts into web pages viewed by other users. Use output encoding libraries or built-in framework features to sanitize and encode user-generated content before displaying it.

```
// Using Razor syntax for output encoding in ASP.NET Core
<p>@Html.Raw(userInput)</p>
```

3. Authentication and Authorization

Implement robust authentication and authorization mechanisms to ensure that only authorized users can access specific parts of your application. Utilize libraries like ASP.NET Identity for user management.

```
// Example of authorization attribute in ASP.NET Core
[Authorize(Roles = "Admin")]
```

```
public IActionResult AdminDashboard()
{
// Only authorized users with the "Admin" role can access this action
// ...
}
```

4. Secure Session Management

Use secure and random session tokens to manage user sessions. Invalidate or expire sessions after a period of inactivity to reduce the risk of session hijacking.

```
// Configuring session timeout in ASP.NET Core
services.AddSession(options =>
{
options.IdleTimeout = TimeSpan.FromMinutes(30);
});
```

5. HTTPS Everywhere

Enforce HTTPS for your web application to encrypt data in transit and protect against eavesdropping and man-in-the-middle attacks. Obtain an SSL/TLS certificate for your domain.

```
// Enabling HTTPS redirection in ASP.NET Core
public void Configure(IApplicationBuilder app, IWebHostEnvironment env)
{
```

```
//...
if (env.IsDevelopment())
{
app.UseDeveloperExceptionPage();
}
else
{
app.UseExceptionHandler("/Home/Error");
app.UseHsts();
}
// Redirect HTTP requests to HTTPS
app.UseHttpsRedirection();
//...
}
```

6. Content Security Policy (CSP)

Implement a Content Security Policy to mitigate the risk of XSS attacks. CSP defines which sources of content are considered valid, reducing the chances of malicious script execution.

```
// Configuring Content Security Policy in ASP.NET Core
app.Use(async (context, next) =>
{
```

```
context.Response.Headers.Add("Content-Security-Policy",
"default-src 'self'; script-src 'self' code.jquery.com");
await next();
});
```

7. Cross-Origin Resource Sharing (CORS)

If your application provides APIs or content that needs to be accessed by other domains, configure CORS to restrict which domains are allowed to make requests to your server.

```
// Configuring CORS in ASP.NET Core
services.AddCors(options =>
{
options.AddPolicy("AllowOrigin",
builder => builder.WithOrigins("https://example.com"));
});
```

8. Regular Security Audits

Regularly conduct security audits, code reviews, and vulnerability assessments of your web application. Use security scanning tools to identify and fix security issues.

9. Error Handling

Implement custom error pages and avoid exposing detailed error information to users. Log errors securely and monitor application logs for suspicious activity.

Securing web applications is an ongoing process. By following these best practices and staying informed about emerging security threats, you can significantly reduce the risk of security breaches and protect your users' data.

Section 16.3: Handling Security Vulnerabilities

Handling security vulnerabilities is a crucial aspect of maintaining the integrity and security of your C# web applications. In this section, we'll explore common security vulnerabilities and strategies to mitigate them.

1. SQL Injection

SQL Injection occurs when an attacker inserts malicious SQL queries into user inputs, potentially leading to unauthorized access or data leakage. To prevent SQL Injection:

```
// Use parameterized queries with Entity Framework to prevent SQL Injection

var query = "SELECT * FROM Users WHERE Username = @username AND Password = @password";

var user = context.Users.FromSqlRaw(query, new SqlParameter("@username", username), new SqlParameter("@password", password)).FirstOrDefault();
```

2. Cross-Site Request Forgery (CSRF)

CSRF attacks trick users into performing unintended actions on a website without their consent. To mitigate CSRF:

```
// Use anti-forgery tokens in ASP.NET Core
```

```
<form asp-antiforgery="true">
<!—Form contents—>
</form>
```

3. Cross-Site Scripting (XSS)

XSS attacks occur when an attacker injects malicious scripts into web pages viewed by other users. Mitigate XSS vulnerabilities:

```
// Use Razor syntax for automatic output encoding in ASP.NET Core
<p>@userInput</p>
```

4. Authentication and Authorization Issues

Ensure strong authentication and authorization mechanisms to prevent unauthorized access:

```
// Use Role-based authorization in ASP.NET Core
[Authorize(Roles = "Admin")]
public IActionResult AdminDashboard()
{
// Only authorized users with the "Admin" role can access this action
// ...
}
```

5. Insecure File Uploads

When allowing file uploads, validate file types and store them in a secure location:

```
// Validate file extensions in ASP.NET Core
[HttpPost]
public async Task<IActionResult> UploadFile(IFormFile file)
{
if (file != null)
{
var allowedExtensions = new[] { ".jpg", ".png", ".gif" };
var extension = Path.GetExtension(file.FileName).ToLowerInvariant();
if (allowedExtensions.Contains(extension))
{
// Process and save the file securely
// ...
}
else
{
// Handle invalid file type
}
}
}
```

6. Sensitive Data Exposure

Protect sensitive data, such as passwords and API keys, using encryption and secure storage practices:

```
// Use secure password hashing in ASP.NET Core Identity

var hasher = new PasswordHasher<User>();

var hashedPassword = hasher.HashPassword(user, "password123");
```

7. Regular Security Patching

Keep your dependencies, frameworks, and libraries up-to-date to patch known vulnerabilities. Use tools like NuGet Package Manager for easy updates.

8. Security Headers

Implement security headers, such as Content Security Policy (CSP) and Strict Transport Security (HSTS), to enhance security:

```
// Configure Content Security Policy in ASP.NET Core

app.Use(async (context, next) =>

{

context.Response.Headers.Add("Content-Security-Policy",

"default-src 'self'; script-src 'self' code.jquery.com");

await next();

});
```

9. Security Testing

Regularly perform security testing, including penetration testing and code reviews, to identify and fix vulnerabilities proactively.

Handling security vulnerabilities is an ongoing process, and staying informed about emerging threats is essential. By following these practices and actively monitoring your web application for security issues, you can protect your application and user data effectively.

Section 16.4: Identity and Access Management

Identity and access management (IAM) are fundamental aspects of securing C# applications, ensuring that users have appropriate access to resources and data. In this section, we'll explore IAM concepts and best practices.

1. Authentication vs. Authorization

Authentication is the process of verifying the identity of a user, often through credentials like usernames and passwords. Authorization, on the other hand, determines what actions a user is allowed to perform after they are authenticated.

In C# applications, libraries like ASP.NET Identity and Azure Active Directory (Azure AD) are commonly used for authentication and authorization.

2. Role-Based Access Control (RBAC)

RBAC is a common approach to authorization, where users are assigned roles, and each role has specific permissions. In ASP.NET Core, you can implement RBAC using attributes like [Authorize(Roles = "Admin")] to restrict access to certain actions.

```
[Authorize(Roles = "Admin")]
public IActionResult AdminDashboard()
{
// Only users with the "Admin" role can access this action
// ...
}
```

3. Claims-Based Authentication

Claims-based authentication associates user attributes (claims) with their identity. Claims can include roles, permissions, and user-specific data. ASP.NET Identity and Azure AD support claims-based authentication.

```
var identity = new ClaimsIdentity(new[]
{
new Claim(ClaimTypes.Name, "john.doe"),
new Claim(ClaimTypes.Role, "Admin"),
}, CookieAuthenticationDefaults.AuthenticationScheme);
await
HttpContext.SignInAsync(CookieAuthenticationDefaults.AuthenticationS
new ClaimsPrincipal(identity));
```

4. Single Sign-On (SSO)

SSO allows users to authenticate once and access multiple applications without re-entering credentials. Azure AD and OAuth

2.0/OpenID Connect are commonly used for SSO in C# applications.

5. Two-Factor Authentication (2FA)

Implementing 2FA enhances security by requiring users to provide two forms of authentication. Libraries like ASP.NET Identity support 2FA through SMS, email, or authenticator apps.

6. Token-Based Authentication

Token-based authentication is prevalent in web APIs. It involves issuing tokens (e.g., JSON Web Tokens, JWTs) to authenticated users, which they send with each request. The server validates the token to grant access.

```
// JWT token generation and validation

var tokenHandler = new JwtSecurityTokenHandler();

var token = tokenHandler.CreateToken(new SecurityTokenDescriptor

{

Subject = new ClaimsIdentity(new[] { new Claim("sub", "user123") }),

Expires = DateTime.UtcNow.AddMinutes(30),

SigningCredentials = new SigningCredentials(new SymmetricSecurityKey(key), SecurityAlgorithms.HmacSha256Signature)

});

var tokenString = tokenHandler.WriteToken(token);
```

7. Access Control Lists (ACLs)

In certain scenarios, you may use ACLs to manage fine-grained permissions for resources. ACLs are typically associated with file systems and databases, allowing you to specify who can access specific resources.

8. Audit Trails

Implementing audit trails helps track user actions and changes in the application. Audit logs can be invaluable for identifying security breaches and unusual activities.

9. Federated Identity

Federated identity allows users to access resources across multiple domains or services using a single identity. Azure AD B2B and B2C are examples of federated identity solutions.

10. Identity Providers

Identity providers like Google, Facebook, and Microsoft are commonly used for external authentication. Libraries like IdentityServer4 facilitate integration with these providers.

Effective IAM is essential for securing C# applications, especially in scenarios where sensitive data and resources are involved. By implementing proper authentication and authorization mechanisms, you can ensure that your application remains secure and compliant with data protection regulations.

Section 16.5: Secure Coding Practices

Secure coding practices are vital for building C# applications that are resilient to security threats and vulnerabilities. In this section, we'll explore key practices to enhance the security of your codebase.

1. Input Validation

Always validate user inputs to prevent common attacks like SQL injection and cross-site scripting (XSS). Use parameterized queries for database interactions and HTML encoding for user-generated content displayed in web applications.

```
// SQL Injection Prevention

string input = userInput;

using (SqlCommand cmd = new SqlCommand("SELECT * FROM Users WHERE Username = @Username", connection))

{

cmd.Parameters.AddWithValue("@Username", input);

// Execute the query

}
```

2. Output Encoding

When rendering data in web applications, ensure that user-generated content is properly encoded to prevent XSS attacks.

```
// HTML Encoding in ASP.NET Core Razor Pages

@Html.Raw(HttpUtility.HtmlEncode(userInput))
```

3. Authentication and Authorization

Implement strong authentication mechanisms, like multi-factor authentication (MFA), and use role-based access control (RBAC) to enforce proper authorization.

4. Password Storage

Store passwords securely using techniques like salted and hashed passwords. Avoid storing plaintext passwords in databases.

```
// Password Hashing with ASP.NET Identity

var hasher = new PasswordHasher<User>();

string hashedPassword = hasher.HashPassword(user, password);
```

5. Error Handling

Implement error handling to avoid exposing sensitive information in error messages. Use custom error pages or responses for different error scenarios.

```
// Custom Error Page in ASP.NET Core

app.UseExceptionHandler("/Home/Error");
```

6. Secure File Uploads

If your application allows file uploads, validate and restrict file types, and store uploaded files in a secure location outside the web root.

7. Session Management

Use secure session management practices, including session timeouts, unique session identifiers, and secure cookie settings.

```
// ASP.NET Core Cookie Settings
services.Configure<CookiePolicyOptions>(options =>
{
options.HttpOnly = HttpOnlyPolicy.Always;
options.Secure = CookieSecurePolicy.Always;
});
```

8. Cross-Site Request Forgery (CSRF) Protection

Implement CSRF protection tokens to prevent malicious requests that could alter user data.

```
// ASP.NET Core Anti-forgery Tokens
<form method="post">
@Html.AntiForgeryToken()
<!—Form fields—>
</form>
```

9. Data Encryption

Encrypt sensitive data at rest and in transit using strong encryption algorithms. Use libraries like Bouncy Castle or built-in .NET cryptography classes.

10. Code Reviews and Testing

Regularly conduct code reviews and security testing, including static analysis, dynamic analysis, and penetration testing, to identify and mitigate security vulnerabilities.

11. Security Frameworks and Libraries

Leverage security libraries and frameworks like OWASP's AntiSamy for input validation and OWASP ESAPI for general security controls.

12. Regular Updates

Keep all software components, including libraries and dependencies, up to date to address known security vulnerabilities.

13. Threat Modeling

Perform threat modeling to identify potential security threats and plan security measures accordingly.

Secure coding practices are an ongoing effort in the software development lifecycle. By integrating security into your development process from the beginning and staying informed about emerging threats and best practices, you can build robust and secure C# applications that protect user data and maintain trust.

Chapter 17: Software Testing and Quality Assurance

Section 17.1: Types of Software Testing

Software testing is a critical aspect of the software development process. It involves evaluating a software application to identify and fix defects, ensure it meets requirements, and guarantee its quality. There are various types of software testing, each serving a specific purpose in verifying different aspects of a software product. In this section, we'll explore some of the most common types of software testing.

1. Unit Testing

Unit testing focuses on testing individual components or units of code in isolation. It ensures that each part of the software performs as expected. Developers typically write unit tests using testing frameworks like NUnit, xUnit, or MSTest. Here's an example of a simple unit test in C#:

```
[Test]
public void Add_TwoNumbers_ReturnsSum()
{
Calculator calculator = new Calculator();
int result = calculator.Add(2, 3);
Assert.AreEqual(5, result);
}
```

2. Integration Testing

Integration testing verifies that different components or modules of a software application work correctly when combined. It checks interactions between these components to ensure they integrate seamlessly. Integration tests help uncover issues related to data flow and communication between parts of the system.

3. Functional Testing

Functional testing examines whether the software application's functionality meets the specified requirements. Test cases are designed to test the application's features and operations to ensure they work as expected. Testers create functional test cases based on functional specifications.

4. Regression Testing

Regression testing involves retesting the software after making changes or updates to ensure that new modifications haven't introduced new defects or broken existing functionality. Automated regression testing helps save time and ensures that previous features still work.

5. Performance Testing

Performance testing evaluates how well a software application performs under specific conditions. Types of performance testing include load testing, stress testing, and scalability testing. Performance testing helps identify bottlenecks and areas where optimization is needed.

6. Security Testing

Security testing aims to identify vulnerabilities and weaknesses in a software application that could be exploited by attackers. Common security testing techniques include penetration testing, code review for security issues, and vulnerability scanning.

7. User Acceptance Testing (UAT)

UAT involves testing the software in a real-world environment by actual end-users or stakeholders. It ensures that the software meets user expectations and business requirements. UAT is often the final testing phase before software is released.

8. Usability Testing

Usability testing assesses how user-friendly the software is. Testers evaluate the software's user interface, navigation, and overall user experience. This testing ensures that the software is intuitive and easy to use.

9. Compatibility Testing

Compatibility testing ensures that the software functions correctly on different devices, browsers, operating systems, and configurations. It's crucial for software that needs to work across a wide range of platforms.

10. Localization and Internationalization Testing

For software targeting global markets, localization testing verifies that the software works well in different languages and cultures. Internationalization testing focuses on designing the software to be easily localized.

11. Exploratory Testing

Exploratory testing is unscripted and involves testers exploring the software without predefined test cases. Testers use their creativity and domain knowledge to find defects and issues.

12. Ad Hoc Testing

Ad hoc testing is informal testing that doesn't follow a structured test plan. Testers perform ad hoc testing based on their intuition and experience, often used for quick assessments or initial defect identification.

13. Alpha and Beta Testing

Alpha testing is conducted by the development team to identify issues within the software before releasing it to a limited audience. Beta testing involves releasing the software to a larger group of external users to gather feedback and identify issues in a real-world setting.

Selecting the appropriate types of software testing and creating comprehensive test plans are essential for delivering high-quality software products. Depending on the project's scope and requirements, various combinations of these testing types may be employed to ensure that the software functions correctly and meets user expectations.

Section 17.2: Writing Unit Tests in C

Unit testing is a fundamental practice in software development that involves testing individual components or units of code to ensure they perform as expected. In this section, we'll explore how to write unit tests in C# using popular testing frameworks like NUnit, xUnit, and MSTest.

Choosing a Testing Framework

C# offers several testing frameworks that facilitate unit testing. Here, we'll briefly introduce three popular ones:

1. **NUnit**: NUnit is a widely used open-source testing framework for C#. It provides a simple and expressive way to write test cases. NUnit supports attributes like [Test], [TestCase], and [TestFixture] to define and organize tests.
2. **xUnit**: xUnit is another open-source testing framework that is gaining popularity. It follows a similar attribute-based approach for defining tests. xUnit offers features like data-driven testing, parallel test execution, and extensibility.
3. **MSTest**: MSTest is Microsoft's built-in testing framework for Visual Studio. It integrates seamlessly with Visual Studio and is a good choice for developers using the Microsoft ecosystem. It supports attributes like [TestMethod] and [TestClass].

Writing Your First Unit Test

Let's create a simple C# class and write a unit test for it using NUnit as an example:

```
using NUnit.Framework;

public class Calculator

{

public int Add(int a, int b)
```

```
{
return a + b;
}
}
[TestFixture]
public class CalculatorTests
{
[Test]
public void Add_TwoNumbers_ReturnsSum()
{
// Arrange
Calculator calculator = new Calculator();
// Act
int result = calculator.Add(2, 3);
// Assert
Assert.AreEqual(5, result);
}
}
```

In this example, we have a Calculator class with an Add method that adds two numbers. We've created a separate class named CalculatorTests to contain our test methods. The [Test] attribute marks the Add_TwoNumbers_ReturnsSum method as a test case. Within the test method:

- We arrange the necessary objects and inputs.
- We act by invoking the method we want to test.
- We assert that the actual result matches the expected result.

Running Unit Tests

Running unit tests can be done using your integrated development environment (IDE) or through command-line tools provided by the testing framework. Most IDEs, including Visual Studio, have built-in support for running tests.

Benefits of Unit Testing

Unit testing offers several benefits, including:

- **Early Detection of Bugs:** Unit tests help identify issues in the early stages of development, making it easier and cheaper to fix them.
- **Regression Testing:** Unit tests serve as a safety net, ensuring that existing functionality isn't inadvertently broken when making changes.
- **Improved Code Quality:** Writing tests encourages writing modular and maintainable code.
- **Documentation:** Unit tests serve as living documentation, showcasing how a component should be used.

- **Confidence:** Passing unit tests provide confidence that the code behaves as expected.

In summary, unit testing is a crucial practice in software development that helps ensure code correctness, maintainability, and reliability. Choosing the right testing framework and writing comprehensive unit tests can significantly enhance the quality of your C# applications.

Section 17.3: Test Automation with NUnit and xUnit

Automated testing is an essential part of the software development process. It allows you to automatically execute tests, check whether the application functions correctly, and identify any regressions quickly. In this section, we'll focus on test automation using two popular C# testing frameworks: NUnit and xUnit.

NUnit

NUnit[1] is a widely-used, open-source testing framework for C# that provides a simple and expressive way to write and run tests. Here are the basic steps for test automation with NUnit:

1. **Install NUnit**: You can install NUnit using NuGet Package Manager in Visual Studio or via the command line using dotnet add package NUnit.
2. **Create Test Fixtures**: In NUnit, you create test fixtures using the [TestFixture] attribute. A test fixture is a class that contains test methods. Each test method is marked with the [Test] attribute.
3. **Write Test Methods**: Inside your test fixture class, write

1. https://nunit.org/

test methods that verify the behavior of your code. Use assertions like Assert.AreEqual, Assert.IsTrue, or custom assertions to validate expected outcomes.

4. **Run Tests**: You can run NUnit tests using various methods, such as the NUnit Test Adapter in Visual Studio, the nunit-console command-line tool, or even within a CI/CD pipeline.

Here's a simple example of a NUnit test fixture and test method:

```
using NUnit.Framework;

[TestFixture]

public class CalculatorTests

{

[Test]

public void Add_TwoNumbers_ReturnsSum()

{

// Arrange

Calculator calculator = new Calculator();

// Act

int result = calculator.Add(2, 3);

// Assert

Assert.AreEqual(5, result);

}
```

}

xUnit

xUnit[2] is another popular open-source testing framework for C#. It follows a similar attribute-based approach for defining and running tests. Here's how to perform test automation with xUnit:

1. **Install xUnit**: You can install xUnit using NuGet Package Manager or the dotnet command-line tool.
2. **Create Test Classes**: In xUnit, you create test classes with methods marked as [Fact] attributes. These methods represent individual test cases.
3. **Write Test Methods**: Inside your test classes, write test methods that assert the behavior of your code. Use xUnit's assertion methods like Assert.Equal, Assert.True, and others.
4. **Run Tests**: You can run xUnit tests using various methods, including the dotnet test command-line tool, Visual Studio Test Explorer, or integrated CI/CD systems.

Here's an example of an xUnit test class and test method:

```
using Xunit;

public class CalculatorTests

{

[Fact]

public void Add_TwoNumbers_ReturnsSum()

{
```

2. https://xunit.net/

```
// Arrange
Calculator calculator = new Calculator();
// Act
int result = calculator.Add(2, 3);
// Assert
Assert.Equal(5, result);
}
}
```

Both NUnit and xUnit are powerful testing frameworks that facilitate test automation in C#. You can choose the one that aligns best with your project's requirements and team preferences. The key is to write comprehensive test suites that cover various scenarios and ensure the reliability of your software.

Section 17.4: Continuous Integration and Continuous Delivery (CI/CD)

Continuous Integration (CI) and Continuous Delivery (CD) are integral practices in modern software development that automate the build, test, and deployment processes. They help ensure code quality, reduce manual errors, and enable rapid and reliable software delivery. In this section, we'll explore CI/CD principles and how they apply to C# applications.

Understanding CI/CD

Continuous Integration (CI)

CI is the practice of automatically building and testing code changes as soon as they are committed to a version control system (e.g., Git). Key components of CI include:

- **Version Control**: Developers commit their code changes to a shared repository regularly.
- **Automated Build**: CI servers automatically build the application from the latest code changes.
- **Automated Testing**: Automated tests, including unit tests and integration tests, are executed to verify code correctness.
- **Immediate Feedback**: Developers receive feedback on the status of their commits, ensuring quick bug detection and resolution.

Continuous Delivery (CD)

CD extends CI by automatically deploying code changes to various environments, such as development, staging, and production. Key components of CD include:

- **Automated Deployment**: Deployments are automated, reducing the risk of manual errors.
- **Environment Parity**: Ensuring that different environments closely match production.

• **Deployment Pipelines**: Defined pipelines that specify how code progresses from development to production.

• **Rollbacks**: The ability to roll back to a previous version in case of issues.

CI/CD Tools for C# Applications

To implement CI/CD for C# applications, you can use various tools and services. Some popular choices include:

1. **Azure DevOps**: Microsoft's Azure DevOps provides a comprehensive set of tools for CI/CD, including pipelines, release management, and integration with Azure services.
2. **Jenkins**: An open-source automation server, Jenkins can be configured to build, test, and deploy C# applications using plugins.
3. **TeamCity**: A CI/CD server by JetBrains, TeamCity offers a user-friendly interface and support for C# projects.
4. **GitLab CI/CD**: If you host your code on GitLab, its built-in CI/CD capabilities can be used for C# projects.

CI/CD Workflow for C# Applications

A typical CI/CD workflow for C# applications involves the following steps:

1. **Version Control**: Developers commit code changes to a version control system like Git.
2. **CI Build**: The CI server automatically triggers a build upon each commit. This build compiles the code and runs automated tests.
3. **Artifact Creation**: If tests pass, the CI server creates deployment artifacts (e.g., compiled binaries).

4. **CD Pipeline**: The CD pipeline takes these artifacts and deploys them to different environments, starting with development and moving through staging and production.
5. **Testing in Each Environment**: Automated tests are executed in each environment to ensure the application behaves correctly.
6. **Manual Approvals**: In some cases, manual approvals are required before promoting code changes to the next environment.
7. **Monitoring**: Continuous monitoring of the application in production to detect issues and respond quickly.
8. **Rollback**: If issues are detected in production, the CD pipeline allows for automated rollbacks to the previous version.

Benefits of CI/CD for C# Applications

Implementing CI/CD for your C# applications offers several advantages:

- **Faster Releases**: CI/CD enables rapid, reliable, and frequent releases of new features and bug fixes.

- **Higher Quality**: Automated testing and deployment reduce the risk of human errors and improve code quality.

- **Consistency**: Environments are standardized, ensuring consistency between development, staging, and production.

- **Feedback Loop**: Developers receive immediate feedback on code changes, allowing for quick bug fixes.

- **Collaboration**: CI/CD promotes collaboration among development, testing, and operations teams.

- **Scalability**: Easily scale the infrastructure and deployment processes as your application grows.

In conclusion, CI/CD is a crucial practice for C# applications that accelerates development, improves code quality, and reduces the time from idea to production. By implementing CI/CD pipelines and using appropriate tools, you can streamline your development process and deliver high-quality software more efficiently.

Section 17.5: Performance Testing and Profiling

Performance testing and profiling are essential aspects of software development that help ensure your C# applications run efficiently and meet performance expectations. In this section, we'll delve into performance testing, profiling, and optimization techniques for C# applications.

Performance Testing

Performance testing involves evaluating how well your application performs under various conditions, such as high load, concurrent users, or specific scenarios. It helps identify bottlenecks, resource utilization, and response times. Here are some common types of performance testing:

1. Load Testing: Load testing assesses how the application behaves under expected load conditions. Tools like Apache JMeter and Microsoft Visual Studio can simulate multiple users and measure response times.

2. Stress Testing: Stress testing evaluates the system's robustness by pushing it beyond its limits. It helps identify failure points and assesses how gracefully the application recovers.

3. Scalability Testing: Scalability testing determines how well the application can scale to handle increased load. It helps in capacity planning and optimizing resources.

4. Concurrency Testing: Concurrency testing focuses on identifying issues related to multithreading and concurrent access to shared resources. It ensures that the application remains stable under heavy concurrent usage.

5. Spike Testing: Spike testing checks the system's response to sudden, extreme increases in load. It helps assess how quickly the application can scale up to meet demand.

6. Benchmark Testing: Benchmark testing compares the application's performance against industry benchmarks or competitors. It helps set performance goals.

Profiling

Profiling involves analyzing an application's execution to identify performance bottlenecks, memory leaks, and areas for optimization. Profilers provide insights into CPU usage, memory consumption, and code hotspots. Some popular .NET profilers include:

- **Visual Studio Profiler**: Included in Microsoft Visual Studio, this profiler offers in-depth insights into code performance and memory usage.

- **JetBrains dotTrace**: dotTrace is a standalone profiler that provides detailed performance analysis and supports various .NET application types.

- **ANTS Performance Profiler**: Developed by Redgate, ANTS Profiler helps pinpoint performance bottlenecks and memory issues.

Optimization Techniques

Once performance issues are identified, optimization techniques can be applied to improve your C# application's performance. Here are some common optimization strategies:

1. Algorithmic Optimization: Review and optimize algorithms and data structures to reduce computational complexity.

2. Memory Management: Minimize memory usage by disposing of objects properly, using object pooling, and reducing unnecessary allocations.

3. Concurrency Control: Ensure proper synchronization and locking mechanisms to prevent contention and deadlock issues.

4. Database Optimization: Optimize database queries, use appropriate indexing, and consider caching strategies.

5. Parallelism: Leverage parallel programming techniques like Task Parallel Library (TPL) and Parallel LINQ to utilize multicore processors effectively.

6. Code Profiling: Continuously profile your application to identify and address performance bottlenecks.

7. Caching: Implement caching mechanisms to store and retrieve frequently accessed data.

8. Compression: Use data compression techniques to reduce network and storage overhead.

9. Content Delivery Networks (CDNs): Offload static assets to CDNs to reduce server load and improve response times.

10. Load Balancing: Distribute incoming traffic across multiple servers to distribute the load evenly.

Continuous Monitoring

Performance optimization is an ongoing process. Implement continuous monitoring using tools like Application Performance Management (APM) solutions to detect issues in real-time and proactively address them.

In conclusion, performance testing, profiling, and optimization are critical for delivering high-performing C# applications. By systematically testing, profiling, and optimizing your code, you can ensure that your applications meet user expectations for responsiveness and efficiency. Performance testing and profiling should be integrated into your development workflow to catch issues early and deliver software that performs well under various conditions.

Chapter 18: Building Real-World Projects

Section 18.1: Project 1 - Creating a Task Management Application

In this section, we'll embark on a practical journey to build a real-world project using C#. The project we'll undertake is the creation of a Task Management Application. Task management applications are essential for individuals and teams to keep track of tasks, set priorities, and manage their daily work effectively.

Project Overview

Project Name: Task Manager

Technologies Used: C#, Windows Forms

Development Environment: Visual Studio

Key Features:

1. User-friendly interface for adding, editing, and deleting tasks.
2. Task categorization and priority settings.
3. Task list with sorting and filtering options.
4. Reminder feature with notifications.
5. Data persistence using file storage.

Project Setup

Before diving into the code, ensure you have Visual Studio installed, as it provides a convenient development environment for Windows Forms applications. Here's a step-by-step guide to set up your project:

1. **Create a New Windows Forms Project**: Open Visual Studio, and select "Create a new project." Choose the Windows Forms App (.NET Framework) template.
2. **Name Your Project**: Provide a name for your project, such as "TaskManager."
3. **Design the User Interface**: Use the Visual Studio designer to create the user interface for your Task Management Application. Design a form with controls like textboxes, buttons, lists, and dropdowns for task input and management.
4. **Implement Task Logic**: Write C# code to handle task creation, editing, and deletion. Create a class or structure to represent a task, and manage task data using collections like List.
5. **Implement Priority and Categorization**: Add features to set task priorities (e.g., High, Medium, Low) and categorize tasks (e.g., Work, Personal, Shopping).
6. **Add Sorting and Filtering**: Implement sorting and filtering options for the task list based on priority, category, due date, etc.
7. **Implement Reminders**: Integrate a reminder system using timers or notifications to alert users of upcoming tasks.
8. **Implement Data Persistence**: Save task data to a file to ensure data persistence between application sessions. You can use file-based storage, XML, or databases.
9. **Test Your Application**: Thoroughly test your Task

Manager application to ensure it functions correctly and is user-friendly.

Project Enhancement Ideas

To take your Task Management Application to the next level, consider adding the following enhancements:

- User authentication and multiple user support.
- Cloud synchronization for task data.
- Task sharing and collaboration features.
- Mobile app versions for Android and iOS using Xamarin.
- Integration with calendar applications.

Conclusion

Building a Task Management Application is an excellent way to apply your C# skills in a real-world context. It covers various aspects of C# development, including user interface design, data management, and event handling. As you work on this project, you'll gain valuable experience that can be applied to more complex software development endeavors. Feel free to customize and expand the application to match your specific requirements and preferences. Happy coding!

Section 18.2: Project 2 - Building a Social Media Dashboard

In this section, we'll embark on another practical project using C#. This time, we'll be creating a Social Media Dashboard application.

Social media dashboards are tools that allow users to manage multiple social media accounts, schedule posts, and view analytics from a single interface.

Project Overview

Project Name: Social Media Dashboard

Technologies Used: C#, Windows Presentation Foundation (WPF)

Development Environment: Visual Studio

Key Features:

1. Integration with popular social media platforms (e.g., Facebook, Twitter, Instagram).
2. Ability to post, schedule, and manage social media content.
3. Analytics and insights for social media accounts.
4. User authentication and account linking.
5. Responsive and user-friendly interface.

Project Setup

Before we dive into the project, make sure you have Visual Studio installed, as we'll be using WPF for this application. Here are the steps to set up your project:

1. **Create a New WPF Project**: Open Visual Studio, and select "Create a new project." Choose the WPF App (.NET Framework) template.
2. **Name Your Project**: Provide a name for your project, such

as "SocialMediaDashboard."

3. **Design the User Interface**: Utilize the Visual Studio designer to create a modern and responsive user interface for your Social Media Dashboard. Design multiple screens for account login, dashboard view, content scheduling, and analytics.
4. **Implement Social Media Integration**: Integrate with the APIs of the social media platforms you want to support. Each platform typically requires its authentication process. Use libraries like RestSharp or HttpClient for making API requests.
5. **Create User Authentication**: Implement user authentication and account linking to connect the user's social media accounts to the dashboard.
6. **Post and Schedule Content**: Develop features that allow users to create and schedule social media posts. Implement a calendar view for scheduling posts in advance.
7. **Fetch Analytics Data**: Integrate with social media APIs to fetch analytics data, including engagement metrics, follower growth, and post performance.
8. **Responsive Design**: Ensure that your application's user interface is responsive and adapts to different screen sizes and orientations.
9. **Testing and Debugging**: Thoroughly test your Social Media Dashboard to ensure that it works seamlessly with the selected social media platforms. Handle error cases gracefully.

Project Enhancement Ideas

To make your Social Media Dashboard even more impressive, consider these enhancements:

- Real-time post previews.
- Integration with additional social media platforms.
- Automated content suggestions based on analytics data.
- Visualizations and charts for analytics.
- Mobile app versions for on-the-go social media management.

Conclusion

Building a Social Media Dashboard is a challenging and rewarding project that requires a combination of C# programming skills, API integration, and user interface design. This project will give you hands-on experience in working with external APIs and handling user authentication, which are valuable skills in modern software development. As you develop this application, you'll be able to streamline your social media management and gain insights into the performance of your social media accounts.

Section 18.3: Project 3 - Developing an E-commerce Platform

In this section, we'll embark on another exciting project using C#. Our goal is to develop an E-commerce platform, a complex and feature-rich application for online shopping. E-commerce platforms are the backbone of online retail, and building one will provide you with a deep understanding of building robust, scalable, and secure applications.

Project Overview

Project Name: E-commerce Platform

Technologies Used: C#, ASP.NET Core, Entity Framework Core, SQL Server, HTML/CSS, JavaScript

Development Environment: Visual Studio Code or Visual Studio

Key Features:

1. User authentication and registration.
2. Product catalog with categories and search functionality.
3. Shopping cart for adding and managing products.
4. Secure checkout process with payment integration.
5. Order history and user profile management.
6. Administration dashboard for managing products, orders, and users.
7. Responsive and user-friendly front-end.

Project Setup

Before we dive into the project, let's set up our development environment and project structure:

1. **Create a New ASP.NET Core Project**: Open Visual Studio Code or Visual Studio and select "Create a new project." Choose the ASP.NET Core Web Application template.
2. **Choose the Project Name**: Provide a name for your project, such as "EcommercePlatform."
3. **Select the Web Application Template**: Choose the "Web Application" template with ASP.NET Core and configure

it to use HTTPS for secure connections.

4. **Choose Authentication**: Select the authentication method you want to use. For this project, "Individual User Accounts" is a good choice to implement user registration and login.
5. **Configure Database**: Set up a database connection using Entity Framework Core. You can choose SQL Server or another supported database provider.
6. **Design the User Interface**: Design the user interface for your E-commerce platform. Use HTML, CSS, and JavaScript for the front-end. Consider using a front-end framework like Bootstrap for a responsive design.
7. **Implement Features**: Begin by implementing user authentication and registration. Then, build the product catalog, shopping cart, and checkout process. Finally, develop the administration dashboard.
8. **Payment Integration**: Integrate a payment gateway like PayPal or Stripe to enable secure online payments.
9. **Testing and Deployment**: Thoroughly test your E-commerce platform, including order processing, payment handling, and security. Deploy the application to a hosting environment, such as Azure or AWS.

Project Enhancement Ideas

To make your E-commerce platform stand out and provide a better user experience, consider these enhancements:

- Implement product reviews and ratings.
- Add recommendations and personalized product suggestions.
- Incorporate a live chat or customer support feature.

- Optimize the application for SEO (Search Engine Optimization).
- Enable order tracking and notifications.
- Support multiple languages and currencies for international customers.

Conclusion

Developing an E-commerce platform is a substantial project that covers various aspects of modern web application development, including front-end and back-end development, database management, security, and payment processing. By working on this project, you'll gain valuable experience in building real-world, large-scale applications that serve a wide range of users. E-commerce is a critical domain in today's digital economy, and the skills you acquire from this project can open doors to career opportunities in web development and software engineering.

Section 18.4: Project 4 - Designing a Gaming App

In this section, we'll embark on an exciting journey to create a gaming application using C#. Building a game is not only fun but also a great way to apply your programming skills to create interactive and engaging software.

Project Overview

Project Name: Gaming App

Technologies Used: C#, Unity (Game Development Engine)

Development Environment: Unity, Visual Studio (for scripting)

Key Features:

1. A simple 2D game with player controls.
2. Game physics, collision detection, and scoring system.
3. Graphics and animations for game elements.
4. Sound effects and music.
5. Menu and game over screens.

Project Setup

To get started with this project, follow these steps:

1. **Install Unity**: If you haven't already, download and install Unity, a powerful game development engine. Unity provides a user-friendly interface for designing and developing games.
2. **Create a New Unity Project**: Open Unity and create a new 2D project. Choose a suitable project name and location.
3. **Design Game Assets**: Design or import game assets such as characters, obstacles, backgrounds, and collectibles. Unity supports various image formats.
4. **Set Up the Game Scene**: Create a game scene and add your game assets to it. Set up the game environment, including the background and any platforms or obstacles.

5. **Scripting in C#**: Unity uses C# for scripting. Write C# scripts to control player movement, handle collisions, manage game logic, and keep score. You can use Visual Studio for coding.
6. **Implement Game Logic**: Implement game logic, including player controls, game physics, and collision detection. Design your game to have a clear objective and win/lose conditions.
7. **Add Animations and Audio**: Enhance your game with animations for character movements and interactions. Incorporate sound effects and background music to make the game more immersive.
8. **Testing and Debugging**: Test your game thoroughly to ensure it functions as expected. Debug any issues in the game's behavior.
9. **Build and Deploy**: Once your game is complete, build it for your target platform (e.g., Windows, Android, iOS) and deploy it for others to play.

Project Enhancement Ideas

To take your gaming app to the next level, consider these enhancements:

- Multiple levels with increasing difficulty.
- Leaderboards to compare scores with other players.
- Power-ups and special abilities for the player character.
- Implement touch or accelerometer controls for mobile devices.

- Add social sharing features to encourage players to share their achievements.

Conclusion

Creating a gaming app is an exciting way to apply your C# programming skills and unleash your creativity. While this project is more focused on game development, it also provides valuable experience in handling user input, physics, animations, and audio integration, which are skills that can be applied to a wide range of software development projects. Building games can be both a rewarding hobby and a potential entry point into the game development industry. Whether you're developing a simple mobile game or a complex desktop game, the principles you learn from this project will serve as a solid foundation for future game development endeavors.

Section 18.5: Project 5 - Building a Financial Management System

In this section, we'll dive into the development of a Financial Management System using C#. Managing finances is crucial for individuals and businesses alike, and creating a software application for this purpose can be highly beneficial.

Project Overview

Project Name: Financial Management System

Technologies Used: C#, WinForms (User Interface)

Development Environment: Visual Studio

Key Features:

1. User authentication and secure login.
2. Dashboard with an overview of income, expenses, and account balances.
3. Income and expense tracking with categories and descriptions.
4. Transaction history and filtering options.
5. Budget planning and tracking.
6. Data visualization with charts and graphs.
7. Exporting financial reports.

Project Setup

Follow these steps to set up the Financial Management System project:

1. **Create a New Project**: Open Visual Studio and create a new Windows Forms Application project in C#. Choose an appropriate project name and location.
2. **Design the User Interface**: Design the application's user interface (UI) with forms, buttons, textboxes, labels, and other controls. Create forms for user registration, login, dashboard, income/expenses entry, and reports.
3. **Database Integration**: Implement a database to store user

data, financial transactions, and budget information. You can use technologies like Entity Framework or SQL Server for this purpose.

4. **User Authentication**: Implement a secure user authentication system with features like user registration, login, password recovery, and session management.
5. **Dashboard**: Create a dashboard that displays an overview of the user's financial status, including account balances, income, expenses, and budget progress.
6. **Income and Expense Tracking**: Develop forms for users to input income and expense details, including categories, descriptions, and amounts. Implement validation to ensure data accuracy.
7. **Transaction History**: Design a transaction history page that allows users to view, filter, and search their financial transactions. Include sorting options and date ranges for better usability.
8. **Budget Planning**: Enable users to set up budgets for different expense categories and track their progress. Visualize budget vs. actual spending using charts or graphs.
9. **Data Visualization**: Implement data visualization using chart controls to provide users with graphical insights into their financial data. Common charts include pie charts, bar charts, and line graphs.
10. **Report Generation**: Add functionality to generate and export financial reports in formats like PDF or Excel. Users should be able to download and print these reports.

Project Enhancement Ideas

Here are some ideas to enhance your Financial Management System:

- Implement financial goals and savings tracking.

- Integrate bank account synchronization for automatic transaction imports.
- Provide alerts and notifications for approaching budget limits or due dates.
- Enable users to set up recurring transactions.
- Implement multi-user support for families or small businesses.
- Add support for multiple currencies and exchange rate conversions.
- Create a mobile app version for on-the-go financial management.

Conclusion

Developing a Financial Management System is not only a valuable exercise in C# programming but also a practical tool that can greatly assist users in managing their finances effectively. This project combines various aspects of software development, including user interface design, database integration, security, and data visualization. It's a valuable addition to your portfolio, demonstrating your ability to create practical software solutions that address real-world needs. Whether you use this system for personal financial management or as a basis for a more complex financial application, the skills and experience gained from this project are highly transferable to a wide range of software development endeavors.

Chapter 19: C# in the Future

Section 19.1: Exploring the Latest C# Features

In this section, we'll take a closer look at the latest features and enhancements introduced in the C# programming language. C# is an ever-evolving language, and new versions bring exciting improvements and capabilities to developers. As of my last knowledge update in September 2021, I'll highlight some of the features introduced in C# 9.0 and C# 10.0, but keep in mind that newer versions may have been released since then.

C# 9.0 Features

1. Record Types: C# 9.0 introduced record types, which are concise and immutable classes primarily used for modeling data. They automatically provide value-based equality and a deconstructor.

2. Pattern Matching Enhancements: Pattern matching received several enhancements, making it more powerful and expressive. Features like relational patterns and logical patterns simplify complex conditional logic.

3. Init-Only Properties: With init-only properties, you can set property values during object initialization, but they become read-only afterward. This is useful for creating objects with immutable properties.

4. Top-level Programs: C# 9.0 introduced top-level programs, allowing you to write simple programs without wrapping them in a class or method. This reduces boilerplate code.

C# 10.0 Features

While I don't have detailed information on C# 10.0 features due to my knowledge cutoff date, I can provide an overview of the direction in which the language was heading based on earlier proposals and discussions:

1. Global Usings: This feature aims to simplify the inclusion of common namespaces by allowing global using directives in all files, reducing redundancy.

2. File-Scoped Namespaces: Similar to global usings, file-scoped namespaces aim to streamline namespace declarations by allowing them to be declared at the file level.

3. Record Types Improvements: Building upon C# 9.0, C# 10.0 might introduce further enhancements to record types, making them even more convenient and powerful.

4. Pattern Matching Enhancements: C# continues to evolve pattern matching with each version, and C# 10.0 could introduce additional patterns and improvements.

5. Nullable Reference Types: Enhancements to nullable reference types may provide more control over nullability annotations, making it easier to work with nullable and non-nullable reference types.

6. Performance Improvements: Each new version of C# often includes optimizations for better runtime performance, making applications faster and more efficient.

To explore the latest features in C#, it's essential to refer to the official documentation and release notes from Microsoft. Additionally, staying up to date with community discussions and blogs is valuable for understanding the practical implications of these language enhancements.

As a C# developer, embracing these new features can improve your productivity and enable you to write more robust and expressive code. Keep in mind that adopting the latest language features should align with your project's requirements and the version of C# supported by your development environment and target platforms.

Section 19.2: Future Trends in Software

Development

As we look ahead to the future of software development, several trends and technologies are shaping the landscape. These trends not only impact how software is built but also how developers work, collaborate, and solve complex problems. In this section, we'll explore some key future trends in software development that are likely to have a significant influence.

1. Artificial Intelligence and Machine Learning (AI/ML)

AI and ML are becoming integral to software development. Developers are leveraging pre-trained models and AI-driven tools to automate tasks, enhance user experiences, and gain insights from data. Natural language processing (NLP) and computer vision are areas where AI is making remarkable progress.

```
// Example of using a pre-trained ML model in C# (ML.NET)

var prediction = model.Predict(new InputData { Feature1 = 0.2, Feature2 = 0.5 });
```

2. Low-Code and No-Code Development

Low-code and no-code platforms are democratizing software development, allowing individuals with varying technical backgrounds to create applications without extensive coding. This trend accelerates application delivery and empowers domain experts to build solutions.

```
// Low-code/no-code platform example

// Build an app through a visual interface without coding.
```

3. DevOps and Continuous Integration/Continuous Deployment (CI/CD)

DevOps practices are becoming standard in software development. Automation, containerization (e.g., Docker), and CI/CD pipelines are streamlining development workflows, improving code quality, and enabling rapid, reliable deployments.

```
# CI/CD pipeline configuration (e.g., Azure DevOps YAML)

stages:

- stage: Build

jobs:

- job: BuildAndTest

steps:

- script: |

dotnet build

dotnet test
```

4. Serverless Computing

Serverless architecture, exemplified by AWS Lambda and Azure Functions, abstracts server management, allowing developers to focus solely on code. This trend simplifies scaling and reduces infrastructure management overhead.

```
// Azure Functions example

[FunctionName("MyFunction")]

public static void Run(
```

```
[HttpTrigger(AuthorizationLevel.Function, "get", "post", Route =
null)] HttpRequest req,

ILogger log)

{

// Function logic here

}
```

5. Quantum Computing

While quantum computing is in its infancy, it holds the promise of solving complex problems exponentially faster than classical computers. Quantum algorithms and languages (e.g., Q#) are emerging.

```
// Quantum computing example (Q#)

operation HelloWorld() : Unit {

Message("Hello, quantum world!");

}
```

6. Ethical and Responsible AI

With increased AI adoption, ethical concerns are growing. Developers are expected to build AI systems that are fair, transparent, and accountable. Ethical AI frameworks and guidelines are emerging.

```
# Ethical AI guideline

- Ensure AI models are trained on diverse, representative datasets to
avoid bias.
```

7. Remote and Distributed Work

The COVID-19 pandemic accelerated the shift toward remote work. Distributed development teams are becoming the norm. Collaboration tools and asynchronous workflows are vital for success.

Team Collaboration Checklist

- Use video conferencing for face-to-face interactions.

- Utilize collaboration platforms for shared documentation and discussions.

- Establish clear communication channels and expectations.

8. Cybersecurity and Privacy

With increasing cyber threats, cybersecurity and data privacy are paramount. Secure coding practices, encryption, and compliance with data protection regulations (e.g., GDPR) are essential.

```
// Example of data encryption in C# (using libraries like BouncyCastle)

var encryptedData = EncryptionUtils.Encrypt(plainText, encryptionKey);
```

These trends represent just a glimpse of the evolving software development landscape. Embracing these changes, staying updated with emerging technologies, and continually improving skills will be crucial for software developers to thrive in the future.

Section 19.3: The Role of C# in Emerging Technologies

As we look at the role of C# in emerging technologies, we can see that C# has evolved to remain relevant and adaptable in a rapidly changing technological landscape. While it has a long history primarily associated with Windows development, C# has expanded its reach into various domains and technologies. Here, we'll explore how C# is positioned in some of the most prominent emerging tech trends.

1. Cross-Platform Development with .NET 5+ and .NET 6

C# developers can now build cross-platform applications using .NET 5+ and .NET 6. These frameworks offer support for macOS, Linux, and Windows, enabling developers to target a broader audience. With the introduction of .NET MAUI (Multi-platform App UI), creating cross-platform mobile and desktop apps becomes more accessible than ever.

```
// .NET MAUI example

public class MainPage : ContentPage

{

public MainPage()

{

var label = new Label

{

Text = "Hello, .NET MAUI!",
```

```
HorizontalOptions = LayoutOptions.CenterAndExpand,
VerticalOptions = LayoutOptions.CenterAndExpand
};
Content = new StackLayout
{
Children = { label }
};
}
}
```

2. Web Development with Blazor

Blazor, a .NET web framework, allows developers to build interactive web applications using C#. Blazor WebAssembly runs C# code directly in the browser, eliminating the need for JavaScript in some scenarios. This approach simplifies full-stack development with a consistent language.

```
// Blazor component example
@page "/counter"
<h3>Counter</h3>
<p>Current count: @currentCount</p>
<button class="btn btn-primary" @onclick="IncrementCount">Click me</button>
@code {
```

```
private int currentCount = 0;

private void IncrementCount()

{

currentCount++;

}

}
```

3. Machine Learning with ML.NET

Microsoft's ML.NET framework allows C# developers to explore machine learning and AI. It provides a wide range of tools and libraries for tasks like sentiment analysis, object detection, and recommendation systems, all while staying in the familiar C# environment.

```
// ML.NET sentiment analysis example

var context = new MLContext();

var data = context.Data.LoadFromTextFile<SentimentData>("sentiment-data.csv", separatorChar: ',');

var pipeline = context.Transforms.Text

.FeaturizeText("Features", "SentimentText")

.Append(context.Transforms.CopyColumns("Label", "Sentiment"))

.Append(context.BinaryClassification.Trainers.SdcaNonCalibrated())

.Append(context.Transforms.Conversion.MapKeyToValue("PredictedLal
```

```
var model = pipeline.Fit(data);
```

4. Cloud-Native Development with Azure Functions

Azure Functions, which can be written in C#, are a key part of cloud-native development. They enable developers to build event-driven, serverless applications that scale automatically. C# developers can use Azure Functions to create microservices, integrate with cloud services, and respond to events.

```
// Azure Function example

public static class MyFunction

{

[FunctionName("MyFunction")]

public static void Run(

[HttpTrigger(AuthorizationLevel.Function, "get", "post", Route = null)] HttpRequest req,

ILogger log)

{

log.LogInformation("C# HTTP trigger function processed a request.");

}

}
```

5. Game Development with Unity

C# has been a popular choice for game development with the Unity game engine. Unity allows developers to create games for various platforms, including mobile, PC, console, and VR. The Unity game engine provides a scripting API that uses C# for gameplay programming.

```
// Unity game script example

using UnityEngine;

public class PlayerController : MonoBehaviour

{

public float speed = 10.0f;

void Update()

{

float moveHorizontal = Input.GetAxis("Horizontal");

float moveVertical = Input.GetAxis("Vertical");

Vector3 movement = new Vector3(moveHorizontal, 0.0f, moveVertical);

transform.Translate(movement * speed * Time.deltaTime);

}

}
```

These examples illustrate how C# is well-positioned in various emerging technologies, making it a versatile language for developers who want to explore and excel in these domains. With its adaptability, C# continues to be a valuable asset in the ever-evolving world of software development.

Section 19.4: Community and Open Source Contributions

One of the remarkable aspects of C# is its vibrant and supportive community. The C# community consists of passionate developers, enthusiasts, and experts who actively contribute to the language's growth and development. In this section, we'll explore the role of the C# community and the significance of open source contributions.

1. Open Source Initiatives

C# and the .NET ecosystem have embraced open source development. Microsoft open-sourced the .NET Core runtime, libraries, and the C# compiler, making them accessible to the global developer community. This move encouraged collaboration, transparency, and innovation.

Contributors from various backgrounds and organizations actively participate in improving the .NET ecosystem. They submit bug reports, propose enhancements, and create pull requests to enhance the language and its associated tools.

2. GitHub and the .NET Foundation

GitHub plays a central role in hosting open source C# projects. The .NET Foundation, an independent organization, fosters the growth of the .NET ecosystem by supporting open source projects, events, and initiatives.

Developers can explore, contribute to, and even start their own open source C# projects on GitHub. Popular projects like ASP.NET Core, Entity Framework Core, and Roslyn (the C# compiler) are hosted on GitHub, where community involvement is highly encouraged.

3. NuGet and Package Management

NuGet, the package manager for .NET, has become an integral part of the C# ecosystem. Developers worldwide publish packages on NuGet, which can be easily consumed in C# projects. This ecosystem of packages saves developers time and effort by providing ready-made solutions for common tasks and challenges.

Contributors often publish their libraries as open source NuGet packages, sharing their work with the broader community. This collaborative approach accelerates the development of high-quality software and fosters knowledge sharing.

4. Stack Overflow and Developer Forums

C# developers benefit from the active online communities, such as Stack Overflow and various developer forums. These platforms provide a space for developers to seek help, share knowledge, and contribute to discussions related to C# programming.

Many experienced C# developers actively participate in these communities by answering questions, providing guidance, and sharing their expertise. This collective effort contributes to the growth of C# programming skills among developers of all levels.

5. Local User Groups and Conferences

C# enthusiasts often participate in local user groups and attend conferences dedicated to the language and .NET technologies. These events provide opportunities for face-to-face networking, knowledge exchange, and learning from experts.

Community-driven initiatives, such as user groups and conferences, play a vital role in connecting developers, fostering collaboration, and promoting the latest developments in C# and related technologies.

In summary, the C# community and its commitment to open source contributions are pivotal to the language's continued success and relevance. The passion and dedication of developers worldwide have not only strengthened C# but also enriched the broader software development community. Whether you're an experienced C# developer or just starting, you can benefit from and contribute to this thriving community.

Section 19.5: Preparing for Your C# Development Career

As you approach the conclusion of this comprehensive guide to C#, it's essential to consider how to prepare for a successful career as a C# developer. Whether you're just starting or looking to advance in your career, here are key steps to help you achieve your goals.

1. Continuous Learning and Skill Enhancement

The software development field is dynamic, with new technologies and practices emerging regularly. As a C# developer, commit to continuous learning. Stay updated with the latest C# features, best practices, and industry trends. Explore online courses, tutorials, and books to deepen your knowledge.

2. Build a Strong Portfolio

A portfolio of projects showcases your skills and experience to potential employers or clients. Create diverse projects that demonstrate your ability to solve real-world problems using C#. Include personal projects, contributions to open source, and work-related applications. Make your portfolio accessible online for easy sharing.

```
// Example: Adding a project to your portfolio

public class PortfolioProject

{

public string Title { get; set; }

public string Description { get; set; }

public string TechnologiesUsed { get; set; }

public string GitHubLink { get; set; }

}
```

3. Networking and Collaboration

Networking is crucial in the tech industry. Attend local meetups, conferences, and online forums to connect with other C# developers. Collaboration on projects or participating in hackathons can provide valuable experience and expand your professional network.

4. Contribute to Open Source

Open source contributions not only give back to the community but also enhance your coding skills. Find projects aligned with your interests and expertise. Start with small fixes or documentation improvements and gradually take on more significant contributions.

```
// Example: Contributing to an open source project

public class Contributor
```

```
{
public string GitHubUsername { get; set; }
public string ProjectName { get; set; }
public string ContributionDescription { get; set; }
}
```

5. Master Version Control

Proficiency in version control systems like Git is essential for collaboration and code management. Learn Git commands, branching strategies, and tools like GitHub or GitLab. Employ version control in your projects from the beginning to track changes effectively.

6. Soft Skills Development

Technical skills are vital, but don't overlook soft skills. Effective communication, problem-solving, and teamwork are highly valued in the workplace. Practice these skills to excel in your C# development career.

7. Job Search and Interviews

When seeking C# developer positions, tailor your resume to highlight your relevant skills and projects. Prepare for technical interviews by reviewing data structures, algorithms, and C# fundamentals. Be ready to discuss your projects and problem-solving approaches.

8. Certifications and Specializations

Consider earning certifications like Microsoft Certified: Azure Developer Associate or Microsoft Certified: C# Software Developer. Specializations in areas such as web development, game development, or cloud computing can distinguish you in the job market.

9. Stay Informed and Adapt

The tech industry evolves rapidly. Stay informed about industry trends and technologies. Adapt to changes and embrace new tools and frameworks as they become relevant to your career.

10. Seek Mentorship

Mentorship from experienced C# developers can accelerate your growth. Reach out to mentors in your network or join mentorship programs offered by organizations and communities.

In conclusion, a successful career as a C# developer requires a combination of technical skills, continuous learning, networking, and a proactive approach to professional development. By following these steps and remaining dedicated to your growth, you can embark on a rewarding journey in the world of C# development.

Chapter 20: Conclusion and Beyond

Section 20.1: Recap of Your C# Journey

Congratulations on completing this comprehensive guide on C# development! You've embarked on a journey through the fundamentals and advanced concepts of the C# programming language, and you're now equipped with valuable knowledge and skills. In this final section, let's recap what you've learned and reflect on your journey.

1. Getting Started

You began your C# journey by installing the necessary tools and setting up your development environment. You wrote your first "Hello, World!" program, gaining confidence in the basics of C# syntax.

2. Core Language Features

You delved into C# language fundamentals, learning about variables, data types, operators, and control flow. You explored how to make decisions using conditional statements and loops, enhancing your ability to control program flow.

3. Object-Oriented Programming

Understanding the principles of OOP was a significant milestone. You mastered the concepts of classes, objects, inheritance, polymorphism, and encapsulation. You also became proficient in handling exceptions in your OOP code.

4. Advanced Concepts

The journey took you deeper into C# with advanced topics like generics, delegates, events, lambda expressions, LINQ, and design patterns. You learned the importance of unit testing and test-driven development.

5. GUI Applications

You explored Windows Forms for building desktop applications, creating user interfaces, handling events, and building complete GUI applications.

6. Cross-Platform Development

You expanded your horizons with cross-platform development using .NET Core, developing console apps, desktop apps, web apps with ASP.NET Core, and even mobile apps with Xamarin.

7. File Handling and Serialization

Working with files, streams, serialization, XML, JSON, and ADO.NET broadened your skills in data management.

8. Networking and Web Services

You gained expertise in networking, building RESTful web services, consuming web APIs, and understanding asynchronous programming.

9. Multithreading and Parallelism

Multithreading concepts, Task Parallel Library (TPL), synchronization, and handling concurrency challenges enhanced your ability to create efficient and responsive applications.

10. Advanced Topics

You explored dynamic programming, reflection, interoperability with native code, advanced debugging techniques, and best practices for performance optimization.

11. Desktop and Mobile App Development

Building desktop apps with WPF and mobile apps with Flutter opened up new avenues for application development.

12. Working with Databases

You mastered database connectivity, SQL operations, Entity Framework, and NoSQL databases.

13. Web Development with ASP.NET Core

Creating web applications, configuring routing and middleware, using Razor Pages and MVC, implementing authentication and authorization, and exploring real-time applications with SignalR broadened your web development skills.

14. Advanced Web Development Topics

Dependency injection, building RESTful APIs, microservices architecture, containerization with Docker, and deploying to the cloud expanded your knowledge of modern web development practices.

15. Security and Testing

You gained insights into security techniques, handling vulnerabilities, identity management, and writing unit tests. You also explored test automation, continuous integration, and performance testing.

16. Building Real-World Projects

You applied your skills to practical projects, creating a task management app, social media dashboard, e-commerce platform, gaming app, and financial management system.

17. Exploring C#'s Future

In the penultimate chapter, you explored the latest C# features, future trends in software development, C#'s role in emerging technologies, and the importance of community and open-source contributions.

18. Preparing for Your C# Development Career

In this final chapter, you've learned how to prepare for a successful career in C# development, including continuous learning, portfolio building, networking, open-source contributions, mastering version control, developing soft skills, job search strategies, certifications, staying informed, and seeking mentorship.

Your journey through the world of C# has equipped you with the skills and knowledge to pursue a rewarding career, contribute to the developer community, and adapt to the ever-evolving technology landscape. As you move forward, continue to learn, grow, and make a meaningful impact with your C# expertise. Your path to C# mastery is just beginning, and the possibilities are limitless. Best of luck in your future endeavors!

Section 20.2: Continuing Your Learning Path

Congratulations on completing this comprehensive guide on C# development! As you step into the world of C# programming, it's essential to recognize that learning is a lifelong journey in the ever-evolving field of technology. In this section, we'll explore how you can continue your learning path in C# effectively.

1. Explore Advanced C# Topics

While this guide covered a wide range of topics, C# is a vast language with many advanced features. Consider exploring more advanced topics like advanced data structures, concurrency patterns, asynchronous programming, and parallelism. Dive deeper into specific areas that align with your interests and career goals.

```
// Example: Exploring advanced data structures like dictionaries

Dictionary<string, int> ages = new Dictionary<string, int>

{

{ "Alice", 30 },

{ "Bob", 25 },

{ "Charlie", 35 }

};
```

2. Build Real-World Projects

Hands-on experience is invaluable. Continue building real-world projects to apply your knowledge and develop practical skills. Consider open-source contributions, personal projects, or collaborating with others on exciting ventures. Working on projects allows you to encounter and solve real-world challenges.

```
// Example: Creating a personal finance management application

public class ExpenseTracker

{

// Implement your application here

}
```

3. Stay Updated with C# Developments

The technology landscape evolves rapidly. Keep yourself up to date with the latest developments in C# by following blogs, reading books, and subscribing to online communities. Attend conferences, webinars, and local meetups to network and learn from others in the field.

4. Explore C# Frameworks and Libraries

C# has a rich ecosystem of frameworks and libraries that can simplify your development tasks. Explore libraries for web development, data science, game development, and more. Familiarize yourself with popular frameworks like ASP.NET Core, Entity Framework, and Xamarin.

```
// Example: Exploring ASP.NET Core for web development
public class Startup
{
public void ConfigureServices(IServiceCollection services)
{
// Configure services here
}
public void Configure(IApplicationBuilder app, IWebHostEnvironment env)
{
// Configure app here
}
}
```

5. Join Developer Communities

Joining developer communities, online forums, and social media groups dedicated to C# and .NET is a fantastic way to connect with fellow developers, seek advice, and share your knowledge. Engaging in discussions and helping others can enhance your learning experience.

6. Consider Further Education

If you're looking to deepen your knowledge and skills, consider enrolling in courses, pursuing certifications, or obtaining a degree in computer science or a related field. Formal education can provide structured learning and open doors to advanced career opportunities.

7. Master Version Control

Proficiency in version control systems like Git is essential for collaborative coding and managing project history. Learn Git and platforms like GitHub or GitLab, which are widely used in the software development industry.

```
# Example: Basic Git commands

git clone <repository_url>

git add .

git commit -m "Initial commit"

git push origin master
```

8. Develop Soft Skills

Technical skills are crucial, but soft skills such as communication, teamwork, problem-solving, and time management are equally important. These skills will enhance your effectiveness as a developer and open doors to leadership roles.

9. Seek Mentorship

Mentorship can accelerate your learning and career growth. Find experienced developers who can guide you, provide feedback on your code, and offer valuable insights. Mentorship relationships can be incredibly rewarding.

10. Embrace Challenges

Finally, don't be afraid to embrace challenges and step out of your comfort zone. Tackling complex problems and learning from failures is how you grow as a developer. Stay curious and persistent in your pursuit of knowledge.

Remember that your journey in C# programming is unique, and there is no one-size-fits-all path. Customize your learning approach based on your interests, goals, and the opportunities that come your way. Stay passionate, stay curious, and keep coding!

Section 20.3: Contributing to the C# Community

Contributing to the C# community is a fulfilling way to give back, share your knowledge, and collaborate with other developers. In this section, we'll explore how you can actively contribute to the C# community and make a positive impact.

1. Open Source Contributions

One of the most direct ways to contribute is by participating in open-source projects. The C# and .NET ecosystems host numerous open-source libraries, frameworks, and tools. You can contribute code, documentation, or help with bug triage and issue management.

// Example: Contributing to an open-source C# library on GitHub

// Fork the repository, make changes, and submit a pull request.

2. *Write Technical Articles and Blogs*

Sharing your knowledge through technical articles and blogs is an excellent way to contribute. Write about C# best practices, tips, and tutorials on platforms like Medium, Dev.to, or your personal blog. Help others by explaining complex topics in an accessible manner.

'''***csharp***

// Example: Writing a blog post on C# design patterns

public class Singleton

{

// Implement the Singleton pattern here

}

3. Create Educational Content

Consider creating video tutorials, online courses, or YouTube channels focused on C# and .NET. Providing educational content helps newcomers and aspiring developers learn and grow. Share your expertise and help others on their learning journey.

4. Answer Questions on Forums

Engage in online forums like Stack Overflow and Microsoft Developer Community. Answering questions, providing solutions, and helping fellow developers troubleshoot issues is a valuable contribution. Ensure your answers are clear and well-documented.

```csharp
// Example: Providing a code solution on Stack Overflow
public static int Add(int a, int b)
{
return a + b;
}
```

5. Contribute to Documentation

Documentation is vital for any technology. Contribute to official documentation, tutorials, and guides to improve the learning experience for others. Correcting errors, updating content, or translating documentation are meaningful contributions.

```plaintext
<!—Example: Editing documentation for an open-source project—>
## Installation Guide
1. Open the terminal.
2. Run the following command:
dotnet install my-library
```

6. Organize or Speak at Meetups and Conferences

If you enjoy public speaking, consider organizing local developer meetups or speaking at conferences. Sharing your knowledge in person or virtually can inspire and educate others. Connect with the developer community and foster networking opportunities.

7. Mentor Aspiring Developers

Mentoring is a powerful way to contribute. Offer mentorship to aspiring developers, interns, or students. Guiding them through their learning journey and helping them navigate challenges can have a lasting impact on their careers.

8. Collaborate on Research and Innovation

If you're interested in pushing the boundaries of C# and .NET, collaborate on research projects or contribute to cutting-edge innovations in the field. Explore emerging technologies and be part of the community that shapes the future.

9. Organize Hackathons and Coding Challenges

Organize or participate in hackathons and coding challenges that focus on C# development. These events encourage creativity and problem-solving and provide opportunities for learning and collaboration.

10. Be a Supportive Community Member

Lastly, be a supportive and respectful member of the C# community. Encourage diversity and inclusion, help newcomers feel welcome, and promote a positive and collaborative atmosphere.

Contributing to the C# community is not only about code but also about sharing knowledge, fostering collaboration, and building a supportive network of developers. Your contributions, no matter how small, can make a significant impact on the growth and vitality of the C# ecosystem.

##

Section 20.4: Staying Updated with C# Developments

Staying updated with the latest developments in C# is crucial for every developer. The tech industry evolves rapidly, and C# is no exception. In this section, we'll explore strategies for keeping your C# skills and knowledge current.

1. Follow Official C# Channels

Stay connected with official C# channels such as the [C# blog](https://devblogs.microsoft.com/dotnet/), the [C# documentation](https://docs.microsoft.com/en-us/dotnet/csharp/), and Microsoft's [developer portal](https://developer.microsoft.com/en-us/). These sources provide updates on language features, tools, and best practices.

```markdown

```plaintext

<!—Example: Checking for C# language feature updates—>

**Latest C# Feature:** Pattern Matching Enhancements (C# 9)

- Introduced improvements to pattern matching.

- Allows more flexible patterns in `switch` expressions.

#### **2. Read Books and Online Resources**

Keep reading books and online resources dedicated to C# and .NET. Authors often release updated editions to cover the latest features and practices. Blogs, forums, and websites like [Stack Overflow](https://stackoverflow.com/questions/tagged/c%23) are valuable sources of information.

```markdown

```plaintext

<!—Example: Reading a C# book for in-depth knowledge—>

**Recommended Book:** "C# in Depth" by Jon Skeet

- Covers advanced C# features and idioms.

- Keeps readers informed about language updates.

#### **3. Join C# and .NET Communities**

Participate in C# and .NET communities both online and offline. Engage in discussions on platforms like [GitHub Discussions](https://github.com/dotnet/csharplang/discussions), [Reddit](https://www.reddit.com/r/csharp/), and developer forums. Attend local meetups and conferences to network with peers.

#### **4. Explore NuGet Packages**

NuGet is a package manager for .NET that hosts a vast ecosystem of libraries and tools. Regularly search for and explore new packages that can enhance your development process. Package maintainers often update their libraries to leverage the latest C# features.

```csharp

// Example: Installing a NuGet package with .NET CLI

dotnet add package package-name
```

5. Learn from Open-Source Projects

Browse open-source projects written in C# on platforms like GitHub. Studying codebases, reviewing pull requests, and contributing to projects can help you learn from others and keep up with coding styles and best practices.

```
// Example: Reviewing and learning from open-source code
// in a GitHub repository.
```

6. Experiment with Preview Features

Microsoft occasionally releases preview versions of C# features. These previews allow developers to experiment with upcoming language enhancements. Use these previews in non-production environments to explore new capabilities.

```
// Example: Enabling C# preview features in a project.
// <LangVersion>preview</LangVersion>
```

7. Practice Continuous Learning

Treat learning as a continuous process. Allocate time for learning new C# features, trying out different development techniques, and experimenting with code. Create personal projects to apply what you've learned.

8. Collaborate with Peers

Collaborate with fellow developers on projects. Peer code reviews and discussions can expose you to different approaches and coding styles. Learning from others is a valuable part of staying updated.

9. Consider Online Courses

Online learning platforms like Pluralsight, Udemy, and Coursera offer C# courses. Consider enrolling in courses that cover advanced topics, design patterns, or specific frameworks like ASP.NET Core.

10. Embrace Change

Finally, embrace change and be open to adopting new tools and practices. Technology evolves to solve problems more efficiently, so staying adaptable and open-minded is essential.

Staying updated with C# developments is not just about acquiring new skills; it's about maintaining your relevance and ensuring your work remains efficient and effective. By following these strategies, you can continue to thrive as a C# developer in an ever-evolving tech landscape.

Section 20.5: Your Path to C# Mastery

Congratulations on completing this comprehensive guide to C#! You've journeyed through the fundamentals, explored advanced topics, and learned about real-world applications of C#. In this final section, we'll discuss your path to C# mastery and what lies ahead in your development career.

1. Reflect on Your Learning

Take a moment to reflect on your C# journey. Consider the topics you've explored, projects you've built, and challenges you've overcome. Reflecting on your learning experiences can help solidify your understanding.

2. Build a Portfolio

Creating a portfolio is essential for showcasing your skills to potential employers or clients. Share the projects you've developed, code samples, and documentation on platforms like GitHub or your personal website.

```plaintext

***<!—Example: Portfolio entry for a task management app—>***

***\*\*Project:\*\* TaskMe - Task Management Application***

***- Description: A feature-rich task management app built with C# and ASP.NET Core.***

***- Features: User authentication, task scheduling, and data visualization.***

***- GitHub Repository: [TaskMe on GitHub](https://github.com/yourusername/taskme)***

#### **3. Explore Specializations**

C# is a versatile language, and you can choose to specialize in areas like web development, mobile app development, game development, or data science. Identify your interests and explore relevant technologies and frameworks.

#### **4. Contribute to Open Source**

Contributing to open-source projects is an excellent way to gain experience and collaborate with other developers. Find projects aligned with your interests and make meaningful contributions.

```csharp

// Example: Forking and contributing to an open-source C# project.

*5. Consider Certification*

Certifications, such as Microsoft's Certified: Azure Developer Associate[1], can validate your expertise and enhance your credibility as a C# developer.

*6. Stay Informed*

Continuously stay informed about the latest C# features, updates, and industry trends. Subscribe to newsletters, follow tech news websites, and attend conferences to keep your knowledge current.

*7. Mentor Others*

If you've gained substantial experience, consider mentoring junior developers. Sharing your knowledge not only helps others but also reinforces your understanding of C# concepts.

*8. Network and Collaborate*

Networking is crucial in the tech industry. Attend developer meetups, conferences, and online forums to connect with like-minded professionals. Collaborative projects can lead to exciting opportunities.

---

1. https://docs.microsoft.com/en-us/learn/certifications/azure-developer

### *9. Set Goals*

Set clear goals for your C# journey. Define what you want to achieve in the short term and long term. Whether it's mastering a specific framework or landing a dream job, having goals provides direction.

### *10. Keep Coding*

Ultimately, the key to mastery is practice. Keep coding, building, and refining your skills. Consistent effort and a passion for coding will drive your success in the world of C# development.

Your journey with C# doesn't end here; it's a continuous path of growth and exploration. As technology evolves, so do the opportunities for C# developers. Stay curious, keep learning, and embrace the exciting challenges that lie ahead. You have the tools and knowledge to excel in your C# development career. Best of luck on your path to C# mastery!

www.ingramcontent.com/pod-product-compliance
Lightning Source LLC
LaVergne TN
LVHW090301210926
848480LV00001B/93
* 9 7 9 8 2 2 3 3 7 9 5 8 4 *